C0-ASK-886

People of Destiny

A Humanities Series

There comes a time,
we know not when,
that marks
the destiny of men.

Joseph Addison Alexander

Public School Library
No. 67 89498
COLUMBUS, OHIO

People of Destiny

BABE RUTH

By Kenneth Richards

*For her cooperation in reviewing this manuscript,
the editors wish to express
their appreciation to Mrs. Claire Ruth.*

CHILDRENS PRESS, CHICAGO

*The editors wish to express
their appreciation to Mr. Meyer Goldberg,
who created the series and inspired
the publication of* People of Destiny

Cover and body design: John Hollis

Project editor: Joan Downing

Editorial assistant: Gerri Stoller

*Illustrations: Bob Brunton—Hollis
Associates*

Research editor: Robert Hendrickson

*Photographs: From the files of Wide World
Photos, Inc.*

Typesetting: American Typesetting Co.

Printing: The Regensteiner Corporation

*Quotations on pages 17; 18; 19; 20; 21; 23, col. 1, ll. 36-40; 23,
col. 2, ll. 1-3, 17-19; 26; 28; 32; 33; 34; 35; 36; 38; 40; 45; 46;
49, col. 1, ll. 1-3; 49, col. 2, ll. 13-14; 51; 53; 59, col. 1, ll. 33-35,
45-50; 60; 61; 63; 64; 69; 70, col. 1, ll. 21-26; 70, col. 2, ll. 8-14;
72, col. 1, ll. 13-17, 20-24, 28-40; 72, col. 2, ll. 10-17, 27-28, 51-53;
75; 79, col. 1, ll. 31-33; 79, col. 2, ll. 11-27, 30-34; 80, col. 1,
ll. 1-14; 81, col. 2, ll. 3-4; 83; 84; and 91 from the book* The Babe
Ruth Story, *by Babe Ruth as told to Bob Consodine. Copyright,
1948, by George Herman Ruth. Reprinted by permission of
E. P. Dutton & Co., Inc.*
*Quotations on pages 72, col. 2, ll. 29-30; 80, col. 1, ll. 18-20;
80, col. 2, ll. 1-8; 81, col. 1, ll. 10-11; and 86, col. 2, ll. 15-16
from the book* The Babe and I, *by Mrs. Babe Ruth. Copyright ©
1959 by Mrs. Babe Ruth. Published by Prentice Hall, Inc.,
Englewood Cliffs, New Jersey.*
*Quotations on pages 23, col. 2, ll. 9-11; 49, col. 2, ll. 1-3; 59,
col. 2, ll. 17-28; 70, col. 2, ll. 16-21; and 79, col. 2, ll. 38-39 from*
Babe Ruth; The Big Moments of the Big Fellow, *by Tom
Meany. Copyright © 1947 by A. S. Barnes & Co., Inc. Reprinted
with the permission of A. S. Barnes & Co., Inc.*
Quotation on page 86, col. 2, ll. 30-31 from Kings of the Home
Run, *by Arthur Daley. Copyright © 1962 by G. P. Putnam's Sons.
Reprinted with the permission of Putnam's & Coward-McCann.*

*Library of Congress Catalog Card No. 67-26872
Copyright © 1967 by Childrens Press, Inc. All rights
reserved. Printed in the U.S.A. Published simultaneously
in Canada.*

1 2 3 4 5 6 7 8 9 10 11 12 13 14 15 16 17 18 R   75 74 73 72 71 70 69 68 67

Contents

The Sultan of Swat

May 6, 1915, was a Thursday and a sparse mid-week crowd sat in the stands at New York's Polo Grounds to watch a game between the New York Yankees and the Boston Red Sox. The Yankees never did draw much of a crowd in those days and were generally considered a sort of stepchild to the National League champions, the Giants. The Yankees didn't even have a ball park of their own and used the Polo Grounds when the Giants were out of town. Although none of the few fans in the stands that day could have realized it, they were watching baseball history in the making.

Pitching for the Yankees that spring afternoon was a veteran right-hander by the name of Jack Warhop, part Indian and a little fellow as ballplayers go. Facing Warhop for the Red Sox was a big left-handed rookie playing his first full season in the major leagues. His name was Babe Ruth—a lean and hard young man, only twenty years old, but well over six feet tall. The veteran Warhop was well known to the New York fans for his excellent pitching performances in the past. Word coming out of Boston indicated that young Ruth was a hurler of promise and the fans settled back to watch a good old-fashioned pitcher's duel.

For the first two innings it was just that, and the score remained at 0–0 as Ruth came to bat to lead off the third inning for Boston. Pitchers aren't supposed to be great hitters and it may be that Warhop eased up a bit on the rookie. At any rate he put over a pitch that was just a little too good. Ruth's young eyes followed the ball and the massive shoulders twisted in a powerful swing. The strong wrists snapped in perfect muscular coordination and there was a resounding *whack* that echoed around the park. The fans gasped as the ball soared in a sweeping arc to land in the upper right-field stands. A round of applause greeted the youngster as he trotted around the base path with

a grin that stretched from ear to ear. It was his first major-league home run.

On another spring afternoon twenty years later—May 25, 1935—at Forbes Field in Pittsburgh, Babe Ruth, now an aging outfielder, was playing for the Boston Braves. He was forty years old then, his eyes were tired, and he carried some 230 pounds on his still-massive frame. Both he and the fans knew that he was very near the end of his playing career. But if he was virtually unknown on the May afternoon at the Polo Grounds so many years before, in 1935 the name Babe Ruth carried a touch of magic. It was Babe Ruth the fans had come to see.

There was something wonderful in the air that day. Perhaps the gods of baseball were smiling benignly once more on the robust figure of Babe Ruth. In his first time at the plate he clouted a home run and the Pittsburgh fans gave him a generous round of applause as he trotted with his pigeon-toed gait around the bases. In his second time up he whacked still another home run and

this time a greater round of applause followed the grand old man on his round trip. The fans were still murmuring about his performance when he appeared at bat once again.

That time they applauded as he came to the plate—the chances were the old fellow would strike out this time. But the game, the day, and the career of the Babe were not quite over yet. As the Pittsburgh pitcher went into his windup, the tired old eyes suddenly sharpened under a determined scowl. For one brief, glorious instant the old magnificent reflexes returned. The wrist action and the powerful shoulder muscles reacted with an instinct honed and tuned during more than 2000 major-league games. Bat and ball collided with a crash that echoed throughout the park and the fans watched in fascination as the ball contined to rise higher and higher and eventually disappeared over the grandstand roof in right field. It was the only time in history that a ball had cleared the roof in Forbes Field.

The Babe was already rounding first base before the astounded fans caught their breath and began to cheer. By the time he crossed home plate, the stadium was thundering with a roar that some people say could be heard in Wheeling, West Virginia. The gods had smiled, and for a few cherished moments Babe Ruth was once again the "Sultan of Swat"—the greatest home-run hitter of all time.

With a big fifty-two-ounce bat, an awesome natural ability, and an unbridled zest for playing baseball, Babe Ruth met his destiny.

Players watch in fascination as a ball hit by Babe Ruth disappears over the grandstand roof in Pittsburgh. It was May 25, 1935—twenty years after Ruth had hit his first major-league home run. This was the third home run of the day for the aging outfielder, and the first time in history that a ball had cleared the roof in Forbes Field.

"Big George"

On a bright autumn afternoon in 1913, Jack Dunn, manager of the Baltimore Orioles, found himself seated on a bench beside a dusty baseball diamond at the St. Mary's Industrial School for Boys. He had come at the invitation of Brother Gilbert, one of the Xaverian Brothers who managed the training school for orphans, delinquents, and runaways in need of correction and help. There were two games scheduled for that afternoon. The feature game was to be between the varsity team and the alumni of nearby Mount St. Mary's College. But Jack Dunn was here to see the preliminary game among the members of the Industrial School team.

To open the festivities, the school band came marching onto the field filling the air with what they hoped would be recognized as a well-known march. The boys of the school all wore faded blue-denim overalls, and the band was no exception. But the lack of fancy uniforms or musical finesse did not dampen their enthusiasm. Perhaps the most enthusiastic of all was the tall, gangling, moonfaced lad who pounded the bass drum with considerably more ardor than rhythm. His trousers ended well above his ankles and a great shock of black hair threatened to obscure his vision, but he marched along with all the strut and pride of a Sousa bandsman, grinning from ear to ear all the while.

Dunn watched the boy with the bass drum. He studied him with the critical eye of an art collector appraising a painting. Brother Gilbert felt that the boy, George Herman Ruth, had real potential as a baseball player—though he wished the boy had exhibited more enthusiasm for his studies. Dunn, however, knew there was no need for books on the baseball diamond.

In one final blare of horns, crash of cymbals, and thud of the bass drum, the band finished its last number and the leader signaled for the boys to disperse. Placing their instruments carefully under the small stands, the boys whooped and raced for the baseball equipment. The air was quickly filled with whizzing baseballs. The *thwack* of balls being hit to waiting outfielders mingled with the shouts of "I've got it—it's mine" and "Keep those throws low!" Bouncing grounders that kicked up little tufts of dust were scooped up and fired from base to base for imaginary double plays.

Jack Dunn watched as the boys worked out. It was easy to see that the *zing* and *whir* of speeding baseballs was better music to their ears than the notes they had struck with trumpets and trombones. He scanned the group

---

In the illustration at right, Jack Dunn and Brother Gilbert stand in the background watching the boys in the band of the St. Mary's Industrial School for Boys as they prepare to put down their instruments and go to the baseball field. The men are particularly interested in "Big George" Ruth, the boy with the bass drum, whom Dunn had come to recruit for the Baltimore Oriole baseball team.

to find "Big George" and finally found him on the sidelines preparing to throw some warm-up pitches.

Dunn watched closely as the big lad went into his windup. He had a nice, easy overhand motion. After a few pitches, George's arm began to loosen up and he fired the ball with sizzling speed. He was a left-hander and had amazing control for a boy so young. There could be no doubt about it—the lad was good. But Dunn would reserve final judgment until he could see how the boy fared against the batters.

As Dunn watched the warm-up, he thought back to the letter Brother Gilbert had written to him about Ruth.

George Herman Ruth, Dunn had learned, was born in Baltimore on February 6, 1895. He had been named after his father, and people who knew them both said he was a dead ringer for his Dad. Mr. Ruth, of German descent, came from Pennsylvania. George's mother, Katherine Schamberger, was mostly Irish—despite her German name.

The Ruths owned a small saloon somewhere down near the Baltimore docks, and put in very long hours making a living for the family. George was the oldest of eight children, all of whom had died in infancy except for George himself and a sister, Mayme, who was then thirteen. Mrs. Ruth had died the year before, when George was seventeen.

Things weren't easy for the Ruth family. They lived in a small apartment above the saloon and George spent a good share of his early childhood downstairs with the sailors, longshoremen, and waterfront bums. He picked up their coarse language as soon as he learned to talk, and was chewing tobacco by the time he was seven. His parents had very little time for the boy, and he grew up pretty much on his own. He was in trouble much of the time and often found himself before the juvenile authorities for one misdemeanor or another. In June of 1902, when he was seven years old, George's parents brought him to the Industrial School.

He stayed only a few weeks that first time, but by November he was back again and stayed until Christmas, when

once more he returned home. After a two-year absence, George again returned to the school—this time to stay.

By the time Dunn arrived at the school, nearly nine years had gone by and George had reached the age of eighteen. He was a popular boy and was genuinely respected for his athletic abilities. He was studying to be a tailor, and when he turned twenty-one would leave the school to follow his trade.

Brother Matthias, who was umpire of the game that day, had noticed soon after George's arrival at the school that he had tremendous natural talent as a baseball player. Brother Matthias was a giant of a man, six and a half feet tall and weighing 250 pounds. Yet he moved with the grace of a lightweight boxer. He was a quiet man who seldom raised his voice, and George had the greatest respect for him. Brother Matthias had taught George how to play baseball, and he had become something of a hero to the boy.

As Dunn brought his attention back to the boys, the warm-up period was over and the "home" team was taking the field. Brother Matthias signaled for Big George to take a few last warm-up pitches from the mound.

Then the umpire called "Play ball!" and the first batter stepped into the batter's box. He soon went down swinging and a confident grin lit the face of the pitcher. He pushed the shock of black hair back from his forehead, wiped his hands on his blue overalls, and then rubbed-up the ball as he waited for the next boy at bat.

Dunn was impressed with George's curve ball and fast ball. He liked the boy's style. He watched as the second batter was called out on strikes and the third man up popped-up to the shortstop for an easy out. With the side retired one-two-three, Big George trotted happily off the mound as his teammates clapped him on the back.

In the bottom of the first inning, the first man up struck out and the next man drew a base on balls. Dunn was then amazed to see George step to the plate. He couldn't believe the boy was good enough to bat third, for pitchers are rarely good hitters.

Before George Herman Ruth had come to St. Mary's Industrial School for boys (below), he had lived with his family in a small apartment above a saloon. The boy had spent a good share of his early childhood downstairs with the sailors, longshoremen, and waterfront bums (above). He picked up their coarse language as soon as he learned to talk, and was chewing tobacco by the time he was seven.

George took the first pitch for a ball —high and inside. The next pitch was more to his liking, and with an easy but powerful swing he slammed the ball into deep right field for a double. A run scored, and from the grin on George's face one could see he got as much pleasure from a good hit as he did from his pitching performance.

Dunn decided then and there that he would offer the boy a job with the Orioles for the next season.

For the remainder of the seven-inning game, George continued to overwhelm the opposing batters and with the final out had struck out fifteen for a shut-out win. Pleased and jubilant, he came trotting over to the bench where Brother Gilbert had called him to come and meet Jack Dunn.

When Dunn made his proposal that George leave the school and play with the Orioles for the 1914 season, the boy was astounded. It was almost more than he could imagine—to be paid for doing the thing he loved most.

Dunn had to make arrangements for George to leave the school, so he left an amazed, delighted youngster to go and see what he could do. It was several months before Dunn returned, but on February 27, 1914, he came back to sign the papers making him George Herman Ruth's guardian until the boy reached the age of twenty-one. The contract was also signed, and George became a pitcher for the Baltimore Orioles at $600 per season.

The few clothes George owned had been packed for days. He had said a dozen good-byes to every friend in the school. Now, on this cold winter afternoon, the gate of the school was unbarred and he stepped out into a new world and a new life. On his record in the school office a final entry was being written. It read, "He is going to join the Baltimore Baseball Team."

And so began Big George's walk with destiny. Within a few weeks he would acquire a new nickname. Over the next two-score years that name would come to be listed beside nearly every record in the annals of baseball. For Babe Ruth was destined to become the greatest baseball player in history.

Reform School to Red Sox

The trip to the Oriole training camp at Fayetteville, North Carolina, marked the first time young George had been on a train and the first time he had ever left his native city. As the train left the station and gathered speed, George watched the city's buildings fall behind —and with them a life for which he had few fond memories. In the tenement districts alongside the tracks, he glimpsed children playing and brawling in the streets. The scene reminded him once again of his early youth when, neglected and unloved, he had roamed the back alleys of Baltimore. Now, for the first time in his young life, George could view such a scene with detachment. For the first time in his life he was beyond the gates of St. Mary's without being a part of the unhappy, unhealthy environment that he saw through the windows of the speeding train.

George had no room in his makeup for self-pity. And already he had developed the blunt and forthright habit of calling a spade a spade. No excuses, no alibis. In his autobiography, written many years later, he would state simply, "I was a bad kid." He said it "without pride but with a feeling that it is better to say it." But if he felt no self-sympathy he felt a strange twinge of pity and compassion for the waifs he had seen beside the tracks. As the train rumbled southward through Maryland's rolling hills, George made a vow. Some-

Young Ruth, below, is about to board a train for the trip to the Oriole training camp at Fayetteville, North Carolina. This was to be his first train ride, and the first time he had left his native city.

how, someday he would do what he could to help boys who were living as he had lived.

The young rookie sat quietly in his seat as the older members of the team caroused and joked and hashed over old times and incidents of the last baseball season. They were a happy, carefree lot, these ballplayers. George was anxious to become one of the group but he knew it would take time. So he watched their happy-go-lucky antics and grinned at the pranks they pulled on one another. Some gave him a good natured grin or a nod but they were not yet ready to welcome him into the mystic camaraderie that seems to pervade a ball club.

George stayed pretty close to Jack Dunn, who saw to it that the rookie got his meal in the train's dining car. Then after a few more hours of fun and frolic the ballplayers, one by one, began turning in for the night. Young George was among the last to climb into his berth, and as the train clattered through the Virginia countryside he lay for a long while wondering if all this was really happening to him. Finally convinced that it was indeed true, he began to have his first pangs of doubt. Could he really make the grade? At last he fell asleep with the confident words of Brother Matthias ringing in his ears. "I know you'll make it George!"

The next day the Orioles arrived in Fayetteville and were transported to the hotel that was to be their home until they returned to Baltimore for the start of the baseball season. George was thrilled at the new world he found in Fayetteville and, as he would later write, "... walked around wide-eyed all the time." He was especially taken with the hotel elevator—the first he had ever seen or ridden—and he took every opportunity to use this wonderous piece of mechanism. One day, not long after arriving in the hotel, he bribed the elevator operator to let him take over the controls. For the rather naive and unsophisticated rookie, running that elevator was the thrill of his young life. And it very nearly ended then and there! At one floor he forgot to pull his head in and was calling down the hall to one of the players while he started the car up to the next flight. Players yelled at him to pull in his head, which he did just in the nick of time— he barely missed getting it crushed. When he arrived back at the player's floor again, Jack Dunn and several of the older players gave him a heated bawling out. "Just a babe in the woods," one player remarked shaking his head with pity, and the rookie had a new nickname.

Later, on the training field, another player remarked, "Here comes Dunnie and his newest babe." He was referring to the way the rookie trotted after his manager's heels like a young puppy. From then on the name stuck and, by the time Babe Ruth became a household word across the land, few would know or remember that his given name was George Herman.

Jack Dunn was not a hard-driving manager and he liked to start off spring training slowly and gradually increase the workouts. For a while Babe felt a little frustrated. He loved to play baseball as he loved nothing else in the world. Calisthenics and running didn't appeal to him. Ruth was a rangy lad, well over six feet tall, and though he weighed only 160 pounds already showed signs of massive chest and shoulder development. His movements had an easy natural grace that showed the extraordinary muscular coordination and reflexes with which he was equipped. The physical conditioning that was designed to get the "kinks" out of ballplayers after a winter of leisure was a snap for Ruth. He felt it was something of a waste of time and he was anxious to start playing baseball.

At last Dunn began baseball drills. By this time, the Babe had pretty much become "one of the boys," and several of the older players began to take a genuine interest in the likeable youngster. Ben Egan, a catcher who had once been with the Philadelphia Athletics, was Babe's special friend and worked closely with the rookie on the playing field. He gave Ruth his first signs and many pointers such as how to keep the ball hidden so the batter would not get a clue to what type of pitch to expect.

Finally, Dunn scheduled an intrasquad game—the first that Babe Ruth

In Fayetteville, Babe Ruth made up for nineteen years of poor meals. The marvel of it all was that he could consume enough for a half-dozen men, get up from the table, and go to the ball park and pitch seven innings of baseball. Those who witnessed these feats could only shake their heads in amazement.

ever played with professional players. Babe played the first half of the game as shortstop and pitched the last half. On the mound he gave up seven runs but his team won the game 15–9. At the plate, however, the rookie got two hits for three times at bat including his first home run against professional competition. Dunn and the other players were astounded at the homer. Here was a rookie—and a pitcher at that—belting the ball some 350 feet in his very first game. Of course in this age of the "lively" ball, 350 feet doesn't sound like much. But it must be remembered that in 1914 the old "soft" ball was still in use.

Later on, during spring training, the Orioles played the world-champion Athletics in an exhibition game that Ruth pitched and won. In the process he struck out the famed "Home Run" Baker—not once but twice. At this early stage in his pitching career, Babe never worried about who the batter was—they all looked alike to him. Left-handers, right-handers—they were all the same to Ruth and he concerned himself only with getting the ball past them. Later, with coaching, he would learn to pitch differently to each individual.

The eager young rookie was also getting a reputation at another kind of plate—the dinner plate. In later years his capacity for putting away food would become well known and more or less taken for granted. But here in Fayetteville the other players could only watch in amazement as he consumed four or five orders of pancakes and several servings of ham or bacon as a typical breakfast. Whole chickens and custard pies were his normal fare at dinner time. Someone had casually mentioned, on his first day at the hotel, that the food was paid for by the club. Never in his young life had the boy seen such wonderful menus, and he immediately set out to make up for nineteen years of poor meals. The marvel of it all was that he could consume enough for a half-dozen men, get up from the table, and go to the ball park and pitch seven innings of baseball. Those who witnessed these feats could only shake their heads in wonderment.

In April the team returned to Baltimore to begin the 1914 baseball season. On the twenty-second of that month, Babe Ruth pitched his first league game against the Buffalo Bisons. The result was a happy one for the young rookie, as he shut them out with a 6–0 pitching performance. Dunn, of course, was elated, and confidently predicted that if Ruth continued pitching that well he would certainly make it to the big leagues.

It should be remembered that then, as now, the International League was just one step below the majors. It comprised players who had either worked their way up through the other minor leagues or were playing out their last few seasons after a career in the majors. That young Ruth could step out of a reform school and, with no previous professional training or experience, become a winning International League pitcher is nothing less than phenomenal.

Ruth, of course, was elated with his success but then as always he never let it go to his head. With his first paycheck he purchased a bicycle ". . . something that I had wanted and often prayed for through most of my young life," he was to write later. While the older and higher-paid players had automobiles, young Babe rode his bicycle through the streets of Baltimore as happily as if it were a Stutz Bearcat roadster.

As the rookie continued to turn in fine pitching performances, Dunn doubled his salary, and still later in the season raised it to $1800. But as Ruth's fortunes were rising, those of the Baltimore Orioles were starting to skid. In 1914, the newly formed Federal League began making raids on the National and American League teams, offering high salaries to players who would "jump" to the new league. One of the Federal teams was placed in Baltimore and, with many major-league stars playing with them, the fans of the city began to attend the Federal games at the expense of the International League Orioles. Soon Dunn's team was playing to a "crowd" of twenty people while the Feds were packing in thousands. It became necessary for Dunn to sell some of his players to make ends meet for the season. Dunn's misfortune became Ruth's good luck. On July 8,

With his first paycheck, Ruth purchased a bicycle, something he had always wanted, but that until now had not been able to afford. Above, he looks over several that are on display before making his final decision.

1914, the contracts of Babe Ruth and two other players were sold to the Boston Red Sox of the American League. The total amount involved was $8500 of which Babe Ruth was priced at $2900.

Ruth reported immediately to the Red Sox, and on July 11 got his first starting assignment. His first major-league effort was a winning one as he beat the Cleveland Indians 4–3. He went hitless, however, and was removed for a pinch hitter in the seventh inning. In the light of Babe Ruth's later career, it seems incongruous that he was ever lifted for a pinch hitter. Actually, this was the first of only three times in his major-league career that it happened. But it should be noted that he carried only a .250 batting average with him from the International League and manager Bill Carrigan was certainly justified in pulling the eager young rookie.

By early August it was evident that the Red Sox had little chance of capturing the American League championship. The Red Sox owner, Joe Lannin, also owned the Providence Club of the International League and, with Baltimore nose-diving to the second division, there was a chance for the Providence team to win the championship. Ruth was sent down to help bolster the Providence team and also to gain more experience. In the meantime, he had appeared in one other game for the Red Sox, which he lost.

At Providence, Ruth became a regular starting pitcher. The manager of the team was "Wild Bill" Donovan, an ex-major-league pitcher who Babe later described as "one of the finest men in baseball." Donovan took a special interest in the rookie and taught him a lot about pitching that would serve Babe well when he returned to Boston. "He convinced me," Babe wrote later, "that a real pitcher works as if he knows he has eight men behind him." Ruth still liked to go for the strikeouts, and in fact got an amazing 139 in his International League season. But Donovan reminded him, "If you want to last long in this game as a pitcher you've got to remember that your arm is your best friend. Strikeouts count for outs in the box score; but those other outs

at first base or in the outfield count just as much in retiring the side." The rookie listened and learned from the old pro, and just before the end of the American League season he returned to Boston a better-balanced pitcher.

Ruth appeared in two more games for the Red Sox, winning one for a major-league season record of two wins and one loss—a good record for a nineteen-year-old lad in his first season of organized ball. His earned-run average was a respectable 3.91. In the hitting department he managed only a .200 average, getting two hits for ten at-bats. His first major-league hit, a single, came on October 2 against the New York Yankees.

His first, and what was to be his only season in the minors ended with a .231 batting average. He had an unusual extra-base record of two doubles, ten triples, and one homer. His pitching record at Providence and Baltimore for the 1914 season was an exceptional twenty-two wins and nine losses for a percentage of .709—the best record in the International League.

The year 1914 was an historic year. On August 14, the first ship passed through the newly completed Panama Canal. On January 5, Henry Ford had announced a revolutionary plan to pay workers the unheard-of minimum wage of $5.00 per day. On June 28, the Austrian Archduke Ferdinand and his wife were assassinated, and by August, Europe thundered to the sound of guns and marching troops. World War I had begun.

And in baseball, the American national pastime, a new name was being mentioned as the most-promising rookie to arrive in many years. A brash young lad with a big grin, only a few months out of a reform school in Baltimore, was making a name for himself up Boston way. In a few more seasons, after a phenomenal pitching career, he would save the sport from ruin. At the same time, he would drastically change the concept of the game and, in the process, establish records that may stand as long as men play baseball.

Yes, 1914 was a memorable year. And not the least-memorable event was the introduction of Babe Ruth to big-league baseball.

Victory and Frustration

In 1915, the boy from Baltimore became a regular starting pitcher for the Boston Red Sox. By the end of the season he had won eighteen games and lost only six for the best won-lost record in the American League—and the Red Sox won the pennant.

For Babe Ruth it was like a dream come true. His salary for that year was $3500—more money than he had ever dreamed of seeing. And he was earning it by doing the thing he loved most in the world. But he was showing, more and more, a side of his character that would present a problem to his managers throughout his entire career. He enjoyed the carefree night life that he had never known, and now could afford. Bill Carrigan, the Red Sox manager, was only the first of many managers who would grapple with the almost hopeless problem of teaching discipline to Babe Ruth.

Perhaps his disdain for training rules and regulations stemmed from the restrictive years he had spent in St. Mary's. He felt that he was now free, a full-grown man earning his own way, and as long as he performed well on the baseball diamond he felt that no one should be concerned about his personal life. He loved life and had a zest for living as exuberantly off the diamond as he had for playing baseball on it. As he expressed it in his autobiography, "I soon became a kid who took his fun where he found it. But I must have tended to business, too, because I was the American League's won-and-lost leader in my first full season in the loop. No boy who did too much carousing could have won all those ball games."

The Babe would go to any extreme to get a night or weekend on the town. One day in 1915 the club had an open Sunday in Washington. Back in those days, playing ball on Sunday was illegal. Ruth approached Carrigan and mentioned that he would like to visit some of "my people" in nearby Baltimore. The manager gave him the okay and Ruth disappeared until game time on Monday. As he and the manager were walking out onto the field, Babe's father, who was sitting in the stands, yelled down, "How come you don't come and visit us when you're here in the neighborhood, Babe?" Carrigan turned a livid purple at what seemed to him to be a double cross and gave the embarrassed Babe the tongue-lashing of his young life. It apparently had little or no effect, however, as Ruth continued to kick up his heels all the rest of his baseball days.

But in all due justice to the Babe, it must be admitted that he was "up" for every game and the Red Sox indeed got their money's worth of baseball out of the boy.

The pennant race that year was a ding-dong battle from start to finish. The Detroit Tigers battled the Red Sox tooth and nail all the way. The great and ever-aggressive Ty Cobb was having one of his finest years with the Tigers that season and every game between the two teams was a veritable war. The league lead seesawed back

---

On July 8, 1914, Babe Ruth's contract was sold to the Boston Red Sox of the American League. In 1915, the boy from Baltimore became a regular starting pitcher for the Red Sox (opposite). By the end of the season, he had won eighteen games and lost only six for the best won-lost record in the American League—and the Red Sox won the pennant.

and forth throughout the season, but in the final two series between the two teams the Red Sox came out on top.

Both teams were best known for their pitching and defensive play. The Tiger's roster included such great hurlers as Harry Coveleski, George Dauss, and Bernie Boland. The Red Sox, besides Ruth, listed such standouts as George Foster, Dutch Leonard, and Ernie Shore. And to balance the great Ty Cobb, in center field the Red Sox had the one and only Tris Speaker.

Ruth won one of the games played in Detroit in August with the help of Dutch Leonard. It was a grinding 2–1 ball game that finally ended in the thirteenth inning. It was a tough game all the way and there was a great amount of spiking and rough play. Ty Cobb, always noted for his aggressive style and terrifying baserunning, was accused by the Boston writers of everything except manslaughter. By the time Detroit arrived in Fenway Park for the final series of the season, the Boston fans were out for Cobb's blood. This was nothing new for the "Georgia Peach"—in fact he thrived on it. Back in 1910 someone had threatened to shoot him if he ever took to the field again, but Cobb went out and played anyway. In Boston in September of 1915, there was a squad of policemen in center field—just in case.

The fireworks were not long in coming. In one of the games, Cobb felt that Red Sox pitcher Carl Mays had tried

Detroit Tiger outfielder Ty Cobb reaches for a long ball (opposite). The ever-aggressive Cobb had one of his best seasons in 1915, and every game between the Tigers and the Red Sox was a veritable war. The league lead seesawed back and forth throughout the season, but in the final series between the two teams, the Red Sox came out on top.

to hit him with a pitch. This was too much for the fiery Ty and he heaved his bat at Mays. This prompted a free-for-all, with the Babe in the thick of it, of course, and Cobb was thrown out of the game. A police escort was provided to see that Cobb got safely away from the ball park.

All this did not faze Babe Ruth in the slightest—he liked the action hot and heavy. In the final game of the series in Boston he pitched a beautiful ball game and handed the Tigers a 3–2 defeat. A week later the Red Sox clinched the American League pennant and Babe Ruth was headed for his first World Series.

In the meantime Ruth had gotten married. "I felt," he wrote later, "rich enough and old enough (I was 20) to take myself a wife." The girl was a pretty coffee-shop waitress by the name of Helen Woodford who had come originally from Nova Scotia. The young rookie often had his meals in Landers' Coffee Shop where she worked and they began dating when the team was playing at home. One morning over his breakfast coffee, the Babe proposed. As with all things, Ruth used a direct approach in proposing marriage. "How about you and me getting married, hon?" he asked with his characteristic bluntness. Helen was well enough acquainted with Babe by this time not to expect anything more sentimental. She thought it over for a few minutes, weighing the pros and cons of matrimony with the big lovable lug, and then answered yes.

Babe's marriage to Helen was destined to be a turbulent one filled with spats, separations, and tearful reconciliations. But for the budding new Red Sox pitcher of 1915 it meant the hope of a homelife such as he had never known. He immediately began looking around for a farm to buy near Boston. Boston, he felt, would be his hometown for many years to come, and he eventu-ally did buy a farm on the outskirts of the city. But Babe Ruth still had a lot of living to catch up on and the carefree life he enjoyed so much was incompatible with that of a country gentleman. Try as he might, it would still be many years before Babe could overcome his zest for the bright lights and exhilerating escapades to be found in towns and cities across the land.

The Red Sox won the World Series that fall of 1915, beating the Philadelphia Phillies four games to one. But for Babe Ruth it was one of the most disappointing episodes of his life. He was not allowed to pitch in a single game. As he wrote later, "I ate my heart out on the bench."

There seems to be no satisfactory explanation of why Bill Carrigan did not use Ruth in the series. After all, the Babe was the league's won-and-lost leader.

Perhaps the manager felt that the rookie would tighten up under the pressure of World Series competition. He had some of the best veterans in major-league ball to use, so why chance the rookie despite his excellent record? At any rate, it was certainly Carrigan's prerogative as manager to start the pitcher he felt was most likely to turn in a winning performance. But this fact did little to salve the wounded pride and shattered dreams of the young Babe Ruth.

The Babe did get to play, however. In the ninth inning of the first game, with the Sox trailing 3–1, he was sent in as a pinch hitter. The pitcher for the Phillies was none other than the great Grover Cleveland Alexander, but this did not deter the Babe. With two out in the bottom of the ninth, the Sox got a man on first as a result of an error by the Phillies first baseman. At this point, Carrigan selected Ruth to pinch-hit, which was surprising. Not many managers will pick a rookie pitcher as a pinch hitter in a World Series game.

When Babe Ruth was twenty years old, he "felt rich enough and old enough" to take himself a wife. The girl was a pretty coffee-shop waitress named Helen Woodford who had come originally from Nova Scotia. The photograph at right was taken shortly after their marriage in 1914.

Ruth took a healthy swing at the ball and it flew like a shot straight toward first base. This time, the first baseman made up for his previous error by making a spectacular catch, though the ball practically tore his glove off. He easily beat Ruth to the bag and that was the end of the ball game and Babe's participation in his first World Series.

Despite their loss in the first game of the series, the Red Sox came back with a vengeance and won the next four games in a row for the World Championship. Ernie Shore had pitched the losing game and then George Foster and Dutch Leonard came in with winning performances. The next day was a Sunday, so no game was scheduled. Babe, nonetheless, was hoping for the starting assignment on Monday. But Carrigan sent Shore in once more and this time Ernie came through with a fine victory. That made three games in a row the Red Sox had won by identical scores—2–1. The series then moved to Philadelphia, and once more the pitching chores were given to George Foster. By this time Ruth was virtually in tears of frustration. He collared Carrigan that day and asked, "What in blazes does a fellow have to do to get a chance to pitch a World Series game for your club?" Then Carrigan promised Babe he could pitch if the series went into the sixth game. Ruth

For Babe Ruth, the 1915 World Series was one of the most disappointing episodes of his life. As he wrote later, "I ate my heart out on the bench."

was torn between his loyalty to the club and his desire to have the series go into one more game so he could pitch. Oh! how he wanted to wrap up that series with a fine pitching performance. He sat on the bench during that fifth game, cheering for his team and yet silently hoping that somehow there would be one more game. It was a battle right down to the final out, but the Sox won a squeaker with a score of 5–4. Another World Series was now history and the young rookie could only look forward hopefully to the next one.

The year 1915 was memorable not only because it was Babe Ruth's first full year in major-league baseball, but also because it was the year he began hitting home runs.

Ruth knocked in a total of four homers during the 1915 season—a pretty respectable record for those days. The American League home-run leader that year got only seven. Babe hit .315 at the plate, including, besides his homers, ten doubles and a triple. This, no doubt, prompted Carrigan to use him as a pinch hitter in the first game of the World Series.

And so ended Babe Ruth's first full year in the major leagues. If the World Series had been a frustration, he could at least look back with considerable satisfaction to a spectacular season. It would be some time before anyone would give serious consideration to Ruth as a hitter, though most would admit he was about the best-hitting pitcher they had seen in many a year. But there was plenty of talk around Boston about how many games Ruth would win on the mound now that he had a full season's experience behind him.

As for the Babe, the frustrations of the World Series were soon forgotten. With the supreme confidence that was his nature, he looked forward to an even greater season in 1916. In the months before spring training, Babe and Helen lived a happy life with little thought of the future. The off-season would always be hard for Ruth to take—not because he was anxious to set new records but simply because he loved to play baseball. In the meantime, however, he took his fun where he found it.

In Europe, the war grew in ferocity during 1915. The Germans had introduced poison gas to the war and also a new kind of sea warfare—the submarine. The liner *Lusitania* had been sunk by a U-boat with the loss of 1150 lives, including 114 Americans. American relations with Germany and Austria-Hungary were becoming increasingly strained and there was much talk of war around the country. But in baseball circles up Boston way, the talk was of the coming 1916 season.

And what a season it would be!

The Longest Game

Babe Ruth could hardly wait until spring training opened for the season of 1916. This year he would not be wearing the "rookie" tag any longer. He was still the youngest pitcher on the Red Sox roster, having just turned twenty-one in February, but now he had two full seasons of professional ball behind him. The frustrating experience of having to sit out the World Series of 1915 on the bench only made him more determined to prove his worth in the coming year. He trained hard throughout the spring and by the time opening day arrived, he was in splendid physical condition and had added a couple of new pitches to his growing bag of tricks. And he would need them, for this was to be the toughest league in several seasons.

In December of 1915, the Federal League was dissolved and all the star players who had jumped to the Feds were allowed to return to the two major leagues. Great veterans like Eddie Plank, Chief Bender, Ed Roush, Hal Chase, and Joe Tinker went back to the majors, so things were bound to be a lot tougher than they had been in 1915.

The Federal League had been able to coax these stars to "jump" with the offer of high salaries. The American and National Leagues then had had to increase salaries in order to hold the players who stayed. Now there were no more competitive job offers to entice the players and many of the teams began cutting salaries. Ruth was offered the same pay he received in 1915—$3500—but several of the Red Sox players were asked to take cuts. Among those being cut was the great Tris Speaker. The management wanted to cut his salary in half, from $18,000 to $9,000. The "Gray Eagle," as Tris was known, refused to sign, although he went to Hot Springs with the team for spring training. He still hadn't signed when the team left for Boston to open the season, and on opening day Ruth and the other players heard the bad news. Speaker had been sold to the Cleveland Indians for $50,000.

The team was stunned. Tris ranked with Ty Cobb among the greatest ballplayers in the business at the time. As

The "Gray Eagle," Tris Speaker, (opposite)—who ranked with Ty Cobb among the greatest ballplayers in the business at the time—was sold by the Red Sox in 1916 to the Cleveland Indians for $50,000.

Ruth put it later, "As a pitcher I knew what it meant having Tris out there in the outfield." Not only would his great batting and superb defensive playing be missing from the Red Sox, but he would be playing against them during the year.

Soon after the sale was made public, Babe and several of the other team members were talking it over and moaning and feeling sorry for themselves when Bill Carrigan happened to overhear the conversation. He also was going to miss Speaker but he knew they would all have to live with the decision of the management.

Breaking in on the conversation, Carrigan growled, "All right, we lost Speaker! But we're still a tight ball club. We've got good pitching, good fielding, and we'll hit well enough. Now if you guys will stop your blankety-blank moaning and get down to business we can win that pennant again!"

This little pep talk did the trick and soon the Red Sox were back in a winning mood. Babe later recalled how the pep talk affected him.

"I suddenly remembered that the $3780 check I got out of the 1915 World Series was more than my season's pay, and I wanted another to match it. Without Speaker, we hustled even harder!"

And they *had* to hustle. As in 1915, the Detroit Tigers and the scrappy Ty Cobb fought the Red Sox tooth and nail for the league lead until late in the season. Then the wind went out of the Tigers' sails and they dropped further and further behind until they were out of contention. But there was no rest for the hustling Red Sox. As Detroit dropped behind, the Chicago White Sox came on with a rush and in a final dash for the finish line the Red Sox squeaked

through to another pennant victory by a scant two games. Speaker or no Speaker, the busy boys from Boston had pulled it off. They were the American League champions for the second year in a row.

As for Babe Ruth, the big left-hander had compiled the astounding record of twenty-three victories to tie the great Harry Coveleski of Detroit for the most wins in the league. Even if he couldn't claim that honor all to himself, Babe could point with great pride to his fabulous 1.75 earned-run average—the best in the league. And he was indeed proud of that achievement.

"I read not so long ago," he was to write years later, "that I didn't bother with signals; I just had a strong, powerful arm and tried to blow down the hitters by throwing the ball past them. Maybe so, but how do they think I got that 1.75 earned-run average?"

Babe went on to say that Bill Carrigan would never have allowed a pitcher to get away with not following signals. "Bill was a keen student of the strengths and weaknesses of every hitter in the leagues," Babe said, "and he called every pitch thrown. He'd hit the ceiling if any of his pitchers tried to pitch his own game instead of following Bill's game. He could get just about as tough as anybody I ever met. We didn't call him 'Rough' Carrigan for nothing."

To the end of his days, Babe would always be as proud of his pitching performances as he was of the home-run records he later set. He was especially proud of an incident during the 1916 season when, with the bases loaded and none out in a game with the Detroit Tigers, he struck out Ty Cobb, Sam Crawford, and Bobbie Veach in succession to retire the side. That trio represented a one-two-three punch second to none—including the Meusel, Ruth, Gehrig combination of the famed "Murderer's Row" of later years.

The tired but jubilant Red Sox had little time to think about the past season. The World Series of 1916 was upon them and the National League champs, the Brooklyn Dodgers, were waiting to pounce. There could be no doubt that Ruth would get a pitching assignment this year and he was ready and rarin' to go. Carrigan scheduled him to pitch the second game.

The series opened in Boston on Saturday, October 7, and Ernie Shore drew the pitching chores for the Red Sox. With the score 6–1 in favor of Boston in the ninth inning, Ernie very nearly "blew" the game. The Dodgers pushed across four runs before Carrigan sent in Carl Mays to "put out the fire." There was no game on Sunday, but on Monday Babe Ruth got his chance. On that day he pitched a game that stands today in the record books.

The Dodgers' pitcher was a left-hander by the name of Sherry Smith. He and Babe battled it out for fourteen innings—the longest World Series game in history. Babe very nearly had a shutout too. The only run the Dodgers scored came in the first inning. Hy Myers hit what should have been a routine out, or at best a single, but outfielders "Tillie" Walker and "Duffy" Lewis ran into one another while chasing the ball. As both fielders crashed to the ground, the ball rolled out into center field. Before either man could retrieve the ball, Myers had scurried around the bases for an inside-the-park home run.

Babe had the satisfaction of driving in the tying run in the third inning, and from that point on the game became a sizzling duel between two determined left-handers. As inning after inning went by with no score, it began to get dark. Of course there were no lights for night games in those days, and there are some people who say the fourteenth inning shouldn't have been started. But the Babe got the Dodgers out in the top half of the inning and the first Red Sox man up drew a base on balls. Duffy Lewis then laid down a beautiful sacrifice bunt to advance Hoblitzel to second. Carrigan sent in the speedy Mike McNally to run for Hobbie and called on right-handed Del Gainer to pinch-hit. By this time it was very nearly dark but Gainer caught one somehow—people in the stands only heard the crack of the bat—and as the Brooklyn outfield searched desperately for the ball, McNally scooted home with the winning run. The final score was 2–1 and Babe Ruth had won his first World Series game.

"I know it was one of the happiest moments of my life," Ruth wrote later. "I had been waiting for two years to pitch against the National League champions and I think I convinced Carrigan that I could hold them as well as any other pitcher on his staff."

As it turned out, that was Babe's last appearance in that series. Once again he was scheduled to pitch in the sixth game but once again the Red Sox made a sixth game unnecessary. Though they lost the third game 4–3, the American League champs came back to win the next two by scores of 6–2 and 4–1 to wrap up the series.

Babe Ruth was now the toast of the town up Boston way. People would be talking for years to come about that fourteen-inning pitching performance. Fame had at last touched the "Big Fellow," as he was being called, and no matter where he went he was recognized. Messages of congratulation poured in from everywhere, but the one he treasured most was from the St. Mary's School in Baltimore. Brother Matthias and the boys were watching his progress with pride. The kids back there had a new hero—and he was one of their own.

As the World Series ended, the Red Sox received a blow that was to hurt them more than the transfer of Tris Speaker. After the celebration in the clubhouse following the final victory, Bill Carrigan shook hands with all the team, thanked them for their service, wished them luck, and retired from baseball. He was going home to Lewiston, Maine, where he owned a bank. Once more the team was stunned.

Carrigan's retirement came as a real shock to Babe. "It was a big blow to me," he said later. "I not only had a great respect for the man himself, but I had a kid's admiration for a great baseball general. I knew how much he had helped me and in my mind began wondering how well I would succeed under another manager." But baseball greatness was Babe Ruth's destiny, and even without Bill Carrigan the coming years would disprove any doubts he may have had about his future.

Another blow fell on the Boston Red Sox as the year 1916 drew to a close, although its repercussions would not be felt for a few years. Just before Christmas, Red Sox owner Joe Lannin sold the club to a New York theatrical producer named Harry Frazee. The trouble with Frazee was that he was a theatrical man first and a baseball man second. He was one of the big names in show business at the time, but he knew nothing about baseball. In a few years his greater interest in the theatrical world would have a major effect on the baseball career of Babe Ruth.

Meanwhile, during 1916, the rest of the world remained in turmoil. The war in Europe continued to grow in intensity as more and more nations hurled their armies into the conflict. Germany declared war on Portugal, the Russians invaded Persia, Rumania entered the war on the side of the Allies, and Italy declared war on Germany. In Ireland, following the great Easter Rebellion, Patrick Pearse and Sir Roger Casement were hanged as leaders of the ill-fated insurrection. In America, President Wilson was reelected to a second term, running on the slogan, "He kept us out of the war!" In the meantime, however, Wilson had sent General John J. Pershing into Mexico to chase after the infamous bandit Pancho Villa. Though he would never catch the Mexican *bandido*, Pershing would soon earn fame on the battlefields of Europe.

For Babe Ruth, the war in Europe was a distant thing and as the year 1917 dawned, his mind, as usual, was on the coming baseball season. He knew great things were expected of him again by the fans in Boston and elsewhere in the American League circuit. He was a little concerned over how he would get along with and perform under a new manager.

Owner Harry Frazee tried vainly to get the competent and popular "Rough" Carrigan back for at least one more season, but Bill's mind was made up. Failing in this, Frazee promoted the Red Sox second baseman, Jack Barry, to the position of manager. Jack was a veteran ballplayer and former star of the Philadelphia Athletics. He was a popular fellow with his teammates, and besides being a college educated man, he had received a liberal baseball education under the great Connie Mack.

Babe would miss Carrigan, but he liked Barry and knew they could work well together. The rest of the team worked hard also and they staged a nip and tuck battle with the Chicago White Sox for the league lead. Then about Labor Day they began to falter and lose ground. Barry just couldn't seem to whip them to further efforts as Carrigan had done, and the White Sox began to pull away. The season ended with the Red Sox in second place, a full nine games behind the Chicagoans, who won their first pennant since 1906.

For Babe, not being in another World Series was a disappointment. But the Boston fans could not be disappointed in Babe Ruth. For the second year in a row he had won twenty-three games. He appeared in fifty-two games that year, forty-one of them as a pitcher,

and at the plate he earned an imposing .325 batting average. There was now no doubt about it—Babe Ruth was a great ballplayer under any manager.

That year, 1917, marked the first of many altercations Ruth was to have with umpires. It also marked the first and last time he ever struck one. The incident occurred on June 23 of that year and the game made baseball history—not because of Ruth socking the umpire but as an indirect result of it.

The explosion came in the first inning of a game with the Washington Senators, as umpire Brick Owens called four straight balls on Ruth. The Babe blew his top and came storming into the plate to come nose to nose with Owens, at the same time letting the umpire know how he felt in no uncertain terms. Owens was not one to back down easily and he told the Babe to shut up or he'd put him out of the game.

"Throw me out of this game and I'll punch you right on the jaw," Babe screamed.

Undeterred, the umpire stared coldly back at Ruth and said quietly, "You're out of this game right now," and gave the familiar sign with his thumb.

Without a second thought Ruth hit him. "It wasn't a love pat," he recalled later, "I really socked him—right on the jaw. That game is in the record books today, but I'm glad my part in it isn't mentioned."

Babe's teammates pulled them apart and hustled the irate pitcher to the clubhouse. As a result, Ruth was suspended for ten days and fined $100 by the American League president. The fine didn't hurt Ruth too much, but sitting on the bench for ten straight days was sheer agony to a man who

The year 1917 marked the first of many altercations Ruth was to have with umpires. It also marked the first and last time he ever struck one. The Babe blew his top when umpire Brick Owens called four straight balls on him. He came storming into the plate to let the umpire know how he felt. After angry words, Owens threw him out of the game—and at that, Ruth socked him right on the jaw (left).

loved to play baseball. Babe soon came to realize that he had gotten off with a very light punishment.

"They'd put you in jail today for hitting an umpire," he recalled years later. "Ben Chapman, who played with me on the Yankees, and Burleigh Grimes were put out of the game for a year for taking a punch at umpires of a later day."

But the reason that the game made baseball history is for what followed. As soon as Ruth had been ejected from the game, manager Barry called in the great Ernie Shore to take over the pitching chores. With very little warm-up time, Shore came in and retired the next twenty-six batters in succession. Foster, the man Ruth had walked, was thrown out trying to steal and so they gave Shore credit for pitching a perfect game. It was only the fifth perfect game in the history of the sport up to that time.

Babe was proud of a game he pitched in 1917. Early in the year, Tim Murnane, the dean of the Boston baseball writers, died and a benefit game was staged for his widow. It was to be the Red Sox against an all-star team composed of players from the American League. At shortstop there was Rabbit Maranville; in center field, Ty Cobb; Tris Speaker was in left field; and "Shoeless" Joe Jackson in right field. Pitching for the stars was none other than Walter "Big Train" Johnson— who many people rate as the greatest pitcher of all time. Babe himself referred to Johnson as, "the greatest pitcher I ever saw."

The pitcher who got the starting assignment for the Red Sox was a big, twenty-two-year-old left-handed kid by the name of Babe Ruth. For Ruth this was one of the greatest honors of his young life and he pitched as he had never pitched before. He was scheduled to go the first five innings and as he later wrote, "I still don't know how I did it, but I shut them out with three hits." The final score was 2–0 in favor of the Red Sox and Babe would always remember the thrill of shutting out the All Stars.

In April of that historical year, the United States went to war against the central powers of Europe and, once the country was committed to fight, a wave of patriotism swept the nation. "Over There," "It's a Grand Old Flag," "Tipperary," and "Yankee Doodle Dandy" were soon being heard as the top song hits of the land. By mid-summer, American troops were landing in France to take their positions on the Western Front. During the 1917 season a few major-league ballplayers went off to war, but the draft didn't really get rolling until the season had ended. As a married man, Ruth was deferred but he joined a National Guard unit anyway, ready to go if his unit was called.

As the year ended, Babe did not know whether he would be tossing baseballs or hand grenades during the 1918 season. Either way, he would be giving his best performance whenever and wherever he was called. As it turned out, the year 1918 marked an incident that Babe would remember all the days of his life as his "proudest achievement."

In 1917, a benefit baseball game was staged for the widow of Tim Murnane, the dean of the Boston baseball writers, who had died early in the year. Twenty-two-year-old Babe Ruth got the starting assignment to pitch for the Red Sox, who were playing against an all-star team composed of players from the American League. Pitching for the All Stars was Walter "Big Train" Johnson (above, left), rated by many people as the greatest pitcher of all time. At shortstop there was Rabbit Maranville; in center field, Ty Cobb; Tris Speaker in left field; and "Shoeless" Joe Jackson (above, right) in right field.

Birth of an Outfielder

During the winter of 1917–1918, many of the Red Sox players went into military service, including manager Jack Barry. Harry Frazee was faced once more with the problem of finding a new manager. The man he chose to succeed Barry was Ed Barrow, whose name would be interwoven with the story of Babe Ruth's baseball career from that time forward.

At the time of his selection as Red Sox manager, Ed Barrow was president of the International League. He had managed ball clubs before—the Detroit Tigers and several minor-league clubs. He was the man responsible for the "discovery" and development of one of the greatest ballplayers in the game up to that time—Honus Wagner, the "Flying Dutchman." Babe and Barrow were at swords' points almost from the beginning. They were both strong-willed men and clashes were inevitable. In 1947 Ruth sat down and reassessed his relationship with Barrow. Looking back through the years he could view their association without the hot emotions he felt as a youth.

"Barrow was a two-fisted, hard-boiled soul who had built up a reputation in baseball as a man who not only knew how to use his fists but liked the idea," Ruth wrote. "He was hot-tempered and though it was Barrow who helped make me what I became in the game, we had our share of clashes. Barrow was a strict disciplinarian. I was still at the age when I resented anyone pulling the bit too tight on me. As it turned out, we became good friends. We certainly had enough time to mend our differences. Except for 1920, we were together from 1918 until I left the Yankees early in 1935."

Their first clash was not long in coming. On a Saturday in May, just before Memorial Day, the Red Sox wound up a series with the Washington Senators. A holiday doubleheader was scheduled with the Athletics on Monday and the club left Washington that Sunday morning for Philadelphia. Ruth, however, felt a sudden impulse to visit his old hometown of Baltimore and as the train stopped there, Babe hopped off without asking Barrow's permission. By the time Ruth arrived at the ball park just before game time on Monday, Ed Barrow was steaming. Calling all the players together in the clubhouse, Barrow proceeded to give Babe what he later called "the worst bawling out of my entire career."

"It was a double-barreled beaut," Ruth remembered, "He threatened to knock my block off if I ever left the club

---

Babe and Red Sox manager Ed Barrow were both strong-willed men and had many clashes. Their first came in May, 1918, after Ruth had hopped off a train, without permission, to visit his old hometown of Baltimore. By the time Ruth arrived at the ball park in Philadelphia just before game time the following day, Barrow was steaming. He called the players together in the clubhouse and proceeded to give Babe the worst bawling out of his entire career (opposite).

again without permission. I was a hot-head too and yelled that I was going to leave the Red Sox. Like most baseball arguments, it soon died down."

That night Ed called Babe up to his room and they talked things over calmly. Ruth, of course, decided to stay with the Red Sox and went on to have a great season. It was during this 1918 season that a decision by Ed Barrow radically changed the baseball career of Babe Ruth. That decision is largely responsible for the fact that all the great pitching achievements of Babe Ruth are often forgotten when his name is mentioned in this day and age. Ed Barrow took Ruth off the pitcher's mound and put him in the outfield— an action that eventually led to Babe's becoming the greatest home-run hitter in the history of baseball.

The switch, of course, was a gradual thing and Babe appeared in twenty games as a pitcher, winning thirteen of them. The subject of making a hitter of Ruth first came up after a few weeks of the season had passed. One night Barrow called Ruth to his room and

popped the question. As Babe remembered the conversation, Barrow said, "Babe, everybody knows you are a big fellow, healthy and strong. Why can't you take your turn in the box and still play the outfield on days when you're not pitching?" Babe had already developed a real taste for hitting a ball and was always looking for the chance to sharpen his batting eye. He didn't have to take a long time to consider the proposition. "I'll try, Ed, and see how it goes," he said simply.

In any other season, Barrow would probably have been committed to a lunatic asylum for trying to make an outfielder out of a twenty-three-game winner. But with many of the best players off fighting the war, the team was very weak in the hitting department. The practiced eye of Barrow had been quick to recognize the latent talent in Babe Ruth. Starting the day after their conversation, Babe was in the Red Sox lineup every day a right-handed pitcher was used against them.

The season of 1918 was the shortest in the history of the game—the Red

Sox played only 126 games. General Crowder, the United States Provost Marshal, put out a "work-or-fight" order and no baseball games were scheduled after Labor Day. Babe Ruth played in ninety-five games that year and got exactly ninety-five hits, for an even .300 batting average. Included in his hits were twenty-six doubles, eleven triples, and eleven home runs—enough homers to tie with "Tillie" Walker for the American League home-run title. And the Red Sox won the American League championship.

By special dispensation, the two league champions were allowed to play the World Series in early September. The National League champions that year were the Chicago Cubs and the series was scheduled to open in the "Windy City" on September 4. Babe Ruth was given the starting assignment for the Red Sox, and his performances in the 1918 World Series culminated in what he would always point to as "my proudest achievement."

The opening game turned out to be a sizzling pitcher's battle between Babe and the big left-hander, Jim Vaughn, of the Cubs. Both hurlers were at their peak form but Vaughn let down for just a moment and allowed a run in the fourth inning. That was enough for him to lose the ball game, as Babe pitched masterful ball to hold the Cubs scoreless and win the game 1–0. Counting the thirteen scoreless innings he had pitched in the 1916 series, Ruth had shut out National League championship teams for a total of twenty-two consecutive innings. Writers now poured over the record books and discovered that Ruth was within striking distance of the record then held by the mighty Christy Mathewson. In 1905, "Big Six" as he was called, pitched three consecutive shutouts against the Athletics and returned in the 1911 series to hold the same team scoreless for one more inning. The record stood in the books at twenty-eight consecutive scoreless World Series innings. Boston fans were excited at the prospect of their twenty-three-year-old Babe coming home to break Christy Mathewson's record right there in Fenway Park.

Babe's chance came in the fourth game of the series, which was the first game played in Boston. But he almost didn't get to pitch and it is a wonder that he was able to pitch at all. On the train ride from Chicago, Babe, always the big kid, got to wrestling and horsing around with one of the other young members of the team, a second-string pitcher by the name of Kenny. During this roughhousing, Ruth took a swing at Kenny, who ducked, and Babe hit the knuckles of his pitching hand on the steel wall of the car. In a short time the middle finger on his left hand was swollen to three times its normal size and was becoming increasingly more painful.

Barrow was fit to be tied when he learned of the mishap and really gave the sheepish Babe a severe tongue-lashing. But Babe assured him that he would be in there trying the next day no matter what.

At the pre-game workout, Barrow watched apprehensively as Ruth threw some warm-up pitches. Anxious to pitch this game, Babe gritted his teeth and tried not to show the pain that stabbed his hand each time he threw the ball. He must have done a good job of concealing his handicap, because Barrow gave him the nod to start the game.

The swollen finger prevented Babe from getting his proper grip on the ball and he found he was unable to give the ball the right twist as he delivered. But the umpire yelled, "Play ball!" and Babe went to work. He shut them out in the first inning and Cub pitcher George Tyler matched Babe's performance in the last half. The end of two innings saw the score still 0–0, and the third inning came and went with no score on either side. Both the pressure of the game and the pain in the finger began to build up for Ruth, but he hung grimly on. After holding the Cubs scoreless in the top of the fourth, Babe came to bat for the first time with two men on base and two out. He took three balls, a called strike, swung one and

missed, then smashed a 3–2 pitch over the right fielder's head for a triple, driving in two runs and putting the Red Sox out in front. The next man up flied out to retire the side and Babe went back to the mound to continue his quest for a new record.

The fifth inning went by with no score, and then came the crucial sixth. As the Cubs went down without a run, the crowd screamed its appreciation of Babe's performance. He now was tied with Christy Mathewson. A hush fell over Fenway Park in the top half of the seventh and then voices were raised to a screaming crescendo as Ruth got the Cubs out with no runs. The kid had just shattered Mathewson's record and now had twenty-nine consecutive scoreless World Series innings. The record was to stand for forty-three years, until Whitey Ford of the Yankees topped it in 1961.

In the eighth, Babe gave up two runs and the score was tied, but the Red Sox came back with a run in the bottom of

the inning to go ahead 3–2. When Babe walked the first two men he faced in the ninth, Barrow signaled for a new pitcher. Instead of taking Ruth out of the game, however, he sent him to play left field. If the game went into extra innings he wanted the Babe's big bat in the lineup. But reliever Joe Bush got the side out and the win went to Ruth. It was his third pitching victory in World Series competition—and his last.

The Red Sox went on to win the series four games to two and that ended the baseball season of 1918. Two months later World War I ended with the signing of the armistice in a little railroad car near Compiègne in France. Some baseball players were among the 115,000 American boys who were killed in the fighting but the others returned to exchange their military uniforms for baseball "monkey suits" and the coming season promised to be a great one.

During the winter period following the 1918 season, Babe began casting about for ways to earn more money.

A fellow named Johnny Igo suggested that Ruth become a prizefighter. The Babe of course was a big powerful fellow, weighing over 200 pounds, and was in excellent physical condition. He had a reputation for being ready to fight at the drop of a hat anyway—why not fight for pay? As usual, the fearless Babe was ready to try anything once.

After his spectacular season of 1918, Ruth was a well-known name, especially in Boston, so it was fairly certain that the Boston fans would pack any fight arena to see him in action. But instead of starting off with a few warm-up fights, Igo—now Babe's manager—began searching for a big-name fighter to challenge. He finally came up with "Gunboat" Smith, a well-known heavyweight from Philadelphia. The ever-confident Babe okayed the match for $5000, never even bothering to find out who Gunboat Smith was. If he had asked, he would have learned that Smith was an old pro who had been fighting since 1908 and had fought some of the best in the business. He had once beaten the then-current heavyweight champion, Jess Willard, in a twenty-round fight and the year before had fought two four-round fights with an up-and-coming challenger named Jack Dempsey. Babe began workouts in a Boston gym.

In the meantime he was holding out for a $10,000 salary for the coming 1919 season and one day Frazee called him in and signed Babe to a two-year contract at Babe's price. As soon as the contract was signed, Barrow took Ruth aside and told him to "get that crazy idea of fighting out of your thick skull." Babe agreed and the match with Gunboat Smith was called off. It's probably just as well. Big and strong as the Babe was, he would have been no match for the ring-wise and hard-hitting Gunboat.

The Red Sox trained in Tampa, Florida, that spring and it was here that the Babe hit what is generally regarded as the longest home run in history. It came in an exhibition game against the New York Giants at the old Tampa racetrack. "Columbia" George Smith (no relation to Gunboat) was the Giants' pitcher that afternoon and he served up a pitch that the Babe couldn't resist laying into. The ball, which never rose more than thirty feet above the ground, went sailing well beyond the Giants' outfielders and across the racetrack that ringed the field. The awestricken writers in attendance got a tape measure after the game and measured more than 500 feet to where the ball landed and more than 600 feet to where it stopped rolling. A 400-foot homer is a breathtaking event, and it is little wonder that the writers went wild over the power of the big fellow from Boston.

Barrow was still undecided about whether to use Ruth as a pitcher or an outfielder for the 1919 season, but he gave Babe the starting assignment on opening day against the Yankees in the Polo Grounds in New York City. Babe pitched a shutout in that game and for a few weeks he took his regular turn pitching every four days. Besides that, he played in most of the other games as an outfielder. The pace eventually became too strenuous even for Ruth, and Barrow decided to use him every day as an outfielder. Still, Babe pitched enough games to win eight while losing five for the season.

In the meantime he was hitting homers at a record pace. The all-time record for home runs was twenty-seven, a record made way back in 1884 by Ed Williamson of the Chicago White Stockings. The Red Sox played only 140 games in 1919 but that was enough for Babe to shatter the old home-run mark with twenty-nine round-trippers—four of them grand slams. But despite Ruth's performance, the Red Sox nose-dived to

---

After Ruth's spectacular season of 1918, a man named Johnny Igo suggested that Babe become a prizefighter. As usual, the fearless Babe was ready to try anything once. Here he is shown working out with boxing gloves in a gym. Red Sox owner Harry Frazee talked Ruth out of fighting—fortunately for Babe, since the first fight Igo had arranged was with an old pro, "Gunboat" Smith, who had fought some of the best in the business.

sixth place as Harry Frazee began selling off his best players to finance his latest theatrical ventures.

It was during this sorry season that Babe had his hottest clash with Ed Barrow. Babe had slipped into his hotel room at sunup one morning after a night on the town and didn't even have time to get undressed before there came a knock on his door. Jumping into bed fully clothed he had barely time to pull up the covers before Barrow came charging in mad as a hatter. Knowing full well that Babe had just arrived, Ed pulled the covers off him. Finding Ruth fully clothed made Ed all the madder. He gave Babe a real tongue-lashing and then stomped out.

By the time Babe got to the clubhouse that afternoon, he too was in a raging mood over what he considered an indignation. Stalking over to Barrow, who was dressing, Babe called him a name and threatened to punch him in the nose if he ever did that again.

Barrow dared the Babe to repeat the name he called him but Ruth was already sorry for having said it and refused to repeat it. But Barrow was not to be denied.

"As soon as you fellows are dressed," he said to the other players, "I want every man to leave this clubhouse. Ruth will stay here. Then we'll lock the door and see who is the better man."

Babe finished dressing with the other players and then sized up the situation. Barrow was a man of fifty and Babe was only twenty-four. "I had sense enough to realize that I couldn't win, even if I beat him," Babe recalled later. So he left with the other players and went out to the field to warm up. Barrow was still angry, however, and as game time rolled around he informed Babe that he was suspended until further notice. The team won that day, even without Babe, and that night on the train for Boston Babe went around to Barrow's compartment to apologize. Ed accepted Babe's humble and sincere apology and the two never had any further trouble while Ruth remained in Boston.

But the irrepressible Babe would always have his troubles with managers and club owners. He loved the gay life and felt that he was as much above ordinary rules as he was above ordinary ball playing. He had clashes with other players and an occasional squabble with the fans, but he always had an easy and natural rapport with children.

"Kids happen to like me," he said in his later years. "They feel natural around me and I'm the same around them. It isn't just a case of giving out autographs. I've always felt cleaner after a session with kids. Wherever they're gathered, they've turned my thoughts back to St. Mary's and my early days in that institution."

Babe had kept in close touch with his old school and even before he was making big money he frequently sent contributions. Brother Matthias and the boys at the school often wrote letters of congratulation to their hero, and all his life "Big George" remained proud of his school and thankful for the job they had done in turning an incorrigible delinquent into a respectable citizen. As his fame grew, so grew Babe's concern for the millions of children around the country who looked upon him as the greatest sports hero in the world.

The year 1919 drew to a close with Babe playing winter exhibition ball out in California. Fans jammed the baseball parks on the West Coast to see the man who had clobbered the fantastic total of twenty-nine home runs in one season. Most felt it would never happen again.

In January of 1920, Babe Ruth was sold to the New York Yankees. The news fell like a bombshell in the sports world. Babe had been given a few days advance warning of the impending sale but the baseball world in general was astounded. No one then could know the heights that Ruth and the Yankees would reach in the coming decade. It was, in fact, the beginning of a legend.

_____

Babe Ruth had many clashes with managers, players, and even occasionally with fans, but he always had an easy and natural rapport with children. Here he entertains a few of his young friends with stories of his baseball experiences.

Hello New York

As Babe Ruth put it, "They'll never build any monuments to Harry Frazee in Boston." One by one he was selling off the finest players on the Red Sox team. He was becoming hopelessly involved in business debts outside the sport and little by little he was wrecking a championship team. The great outfield of 1915, rated by Ruth and many others as the greatest defensive outfield of all time, was now gone. Pitchers Ernie Shore and Dutch Leonard were sold, and finally the biggest prize of all, Babe Ruth, went to the Yankees. In return for the man who was soon to become the greatest player in the history of baseball, Frazee received $100,000 in cash and a personal loan of $350,000 for which he put up Fenway Park as collateral. As the famous baseball writer Tom Meany once wrote, "All the kings horses and all the kings men couldn't put Boston baseball together again." The Red Sox didn't finish better than fourth again until Tom Yawkey rebuilt the club with the help of Ted Williams' big bat some two decades later.

Ed Barrow, watching in frustration as his team was sold out from under him, expected the worst when Frazee called him long distance one day and asked Ed to meet him at a hotel in New York. "I'll bet 'Frazz' is selling Babe Ruth on me," he told himself. At the meeting his worst fears were confirmed and all his angry protestations were to no avail. Babe Ruth was gone, or soon going, and though Ed probably had no inkling of it then, within a year he too would follow the Babe to New York.

Shown at left is Edward Grant Barrow, manager of the Boston Red Sox. In 1919, Barrow watched in frustration as the Red Sox team was sold out from under him—including Babe Ruth, who was sold to the New York Yankees. Barrow himself was later to join the Yankees as general manager.

The Yankees had rarely been any better than a second division club. But starting in 1915, two colonels, Jacob Ruppert and Tillinghast L'Hommidieu Houston had purchased the faltering New York stepchild and methodically began to build the team into a respectable club of championship caliber. Both were shrewd businessmen, both were wealthy, and both had an all-abiding faith in their ability to put together a winning and profit-making ball team. In 1919 they had worked the club up to a third place finish, and the acquisition of Babe Ruth made prospects for the future look even brighter.

The manager of the Yankees was little Miller Huggins, a pint-sized bundle of dynamite who barely came to Babe Ruth's shoulder. He had been a very good second baseman in his playing days but he was so tiny that Babe Ruth wondered "how such a little guy could have been a good ballplayer. He didn't seem strong enough to swing a bat, or live through a spiking job. But he was a smart little fellow and knew a lot about baseball."

The Babe reported to the Yankee training camp in Jacksonville, Florida, late in February of 1920. From the very start, however, he had trouble getting into the groove. He struck out again and again in exhibition games with the Brooklyn Dodgers, who were training nearby. All the New York writers, who were expecting great things of the newest addition to the team, began to pan the Babe in their columns. Ruth was getting pretty angry at the treatment he was getting in the papers and grumbled one day that he was going to "pop a couple of those newspaper guys if they don't lay off me." Pitcher Carl Mays overheard Babe's remark and gave him some good advice.

"That kind of talk won't get you anywhere, Babe," Mays said. "Those fellows will be only too glad to write something nice about you if you give them something nice to write about. Go out and clip a few homers and you won't have any reason to bellyache about your write-ups."

A few days later the Babe got hold of one with all the power his pent-up frustration could generate. He usually hit to right field but this one went into dead center. The ball was still rising as it passed some thirty feet over the center fielder's head. At last the writers had something spectacular to write about Babe Ruth.

The American League pennant race was a seesaw battle all the way to the wire that year, but the Yankees finished in third place again, only three games behind the first-place Cleveland Indians and one game behind the second-place Chicago White Sox. But the important thing for the Yankees was that Babe Ruth hit the unbelievable total of fifty-four home runs and in the process drew a home-attendance record of 1,289,422 fans who came to see him clout homers. That attendance record was to stand for twenty-six years before the Yankees themselves beat it in 1946. That home-run record affected the fans about the way 150 homers in one season would in this day and age. It was about this time that Ruth acquired the title of "Sultan of Swat," so completely did he eclipse all other ballplayers then playing or who had ever played before. And coming as it did at a crucial moment in the saga of the sport, Ruth's home-run record is credited by many as the phenomenon that saved baseball.

The greatest crisis baseball ever had to face came very late in the 1920 season when it was disclosed that the White

Babe Ruth is shown here playing in an exhibition game at the Yankee training camp in Jacksonville, Florida.

Sox, champions of the American League, had thrown the 1919 World Series. The evidence was irrefutable. The World Series had been fixed by professional gamblers who had bribed certain White Sox players to lose the necessary games to the National League champs. None of the Cincinnati Reds knew of the "fix" and were entirely blameless in the conspiracy as they won the series five games to three, (there were nine games scheduled in those days).

Eight of the "Black Sox," (as they were now called), were indicted by the Cook County Grand Jury in Illinois for conspiring to lose the series and were subsequently banished and blacklisted for life from organized baseball. Among the conspirators was the famous "Shoeless Joe" Jackson, the man whose batting style Babe Ruth had studied and copied. "To me," Babe later recalled, "it was like hearing my church had sold out. I couldn't comprehend how any Big League players could defraud not only the millions of fans all over the country, but millions of kids, by throwing the biggest sporting event of the year."

The reason for the delay in exposing the fraud was that it was difficult to obtain enough testimony and evidence that would stand up in court. But even coming one year after the event, the Black Sox Scandal, when it broke, shattered the very foundations of public trust in the national pastime. Baseball could survive many troubles and ills

---

The greatest crisis baseball ever had to face came in the 1920 season, when it was disclosed that the White Sox, champions of the American League, had thrown the 1919 World Series. At left, "Black Sox" players, as they were now called, leave the hearing room after being indicted by the Cook County Grand Jury in Illinois for conspiring to lose the series.

from mismanagement to lackluster performances, but it could not stand public skepticism and distrust. When Mr. American Baseball Fan paid his money to see a baseball game he had to be assured that he was watching true competition—not a farce. It is generally conceded that the Black Sox Scandal would have sounded the death knell for baseball had it not been for Babe Ruth's mighty bat.

There was nothing fraudulent about the way Ruth swung that big fifty-two-ounce bat. It was direct, honest, and done with such enormous gusto that even his strikeouts were wonderful to watch. He brought a new high drama to a game that, since its inception, had been characterized by bunting, base stealing, and "playing for the one run." The Babe Ruth approach, the home run, was to baseball what the knockout punch of Joe Louis or Jack Dempsey was to boxing—the smashing, final, shortcut to victory. Babe Ruth added a spice and zing to baseball that was typically American in its efficient and expedient method of achieving success. Every time the big fellow came to the plate a tingling expectancy fell over the crowd like the ticking of a time bomb.

It is probably the happiest single coincidence in the history of sports that Babe Ruth really began hitting his towering home runs in steady profusion at the same time the infamous Black Sox Scandal rocked the nation. Because of the Babe, and because other players were beginning to copy Ruth's style, the American baseball fan didn't go sour on the sport in its time of crisis.

As Babe rapidly became the greatest single attraction in baseball, others in the sport were quick to realize that the public craved home runs. The scientific hitters who previously had been punching the ball to "where they ain't" were suddenly swinging for the fences. In the final analysis, it can be said that Babe Ruth exerted the greatest single influ-

ence on the sport in its entire history. The home run changed the concept of baseball much as the pass changed the game of football.

During the 1921 season, more home runs were hit in the major league than in any three-year period prior to 1920. This was partly due to the increased resiliency of the ball. Baseball manufacturers maintained that the ball was never really changed but they admit to several factors that contributed to the so-called "lively ball." Originally, it is said, the yarn used in the manufacture of baseballs came from Australia. This supply was greatly reduced during World War I and ball makers resorted to pure American wool, which—coupled with more-efficient machines for winding the wool—resulted in an improved ball.

It is doubtful that Babe Ruth ever paused to dissect a baseball, but if he had he would have found the design of baseballs exactly alike for both leagues.

The core is a round piece of natural rubber $13\frac{1}{16}''$ in diameter. This is encased within another sphere of rubber $1\frac{3}{16}''$ in diameter and the two are further wrapped in a red rubber casing $1\frac{3}{8}''$ in diameter. This is followed by three wrappings of wool, each of a different texture, and capped with a wrapping of fine white thread. A special cement which binds and hardens everything down to the core is then applied to the whole structure. The final casing is of horsehide, hand sewn with 108 stitches of waxed twine. The yarn is 75% fresh wool and 25% reworked wool, as 100% fresh wool would make the ball too soft. But "dead" or "lively," Babe Ruth was concerned only with knocking baseballs over somebody's grandstand—and this habit stayed with him throughout his baseball career.

One of the countless stories about the Babe concerns a trick ball that someone sprung on him during batting practice one season. The ball looked and felt like

the genuine article, but it was designed so that a batter would be lucky to hit it as far as the pitcher's mound. While the other Yankees stood around grinning, the catcher secretly substituted the trick ball for the real one. The pitcher was in on the prank and he tossed the ball right where he knew the Babe liked to see them. Sure enough, Ruth took a mighty "Ruthian" swing at the ball and, to the complete amazement of the pranksters, the ball sailed out over the second baseman's head and dropped in for a "Texas leaguer"—too far out to be caught by an infielder and not far enough out to be caught by an out-fielder. Their amazement and awe turned to utter glee, however, when Ruth dropped his bat, walked over to his manager and said, "I'm going to have to take the day off, Hug. I'm as weak as a kitten." When they cut Babe in on the little joke they half-expected him to get roaring mad. But as the truth dawned on the Big Fellow he roared with laughter. The biggest practical joker of them all could also appreciate a joke at his own expense.

There were other factors during that early postwar era that led to increased home-run totals. Legislation was introduced that gave an additional advantage to the batters. The emory ball, the shine ball, the spitball, and most other freak deliveries were outlawed. Umpires were instructed to assure that a clean white ball was put into play each time the one in use became soiled or scuffed up. This assured the batter of a nice white target at all times.

In the aftermath of the Black Sox Scandal it became obvious that some sort of guarantee should be given the public that such an episode would never happen again. The club owners decided to put baseball in the hands of a strong, unimpeachable character who could command respect and restore public faith in the sport. The man they finally decided on was a United States District Judge by the name of Kennesaw Mountain Landis.

Upon being approached by the baseball delegation who came to solicit his services, the judge agreed to accept the position—but on his own terms. These terms called for establishing him as an absolute czar with virtually unlimited power to control organized baseball as he saw fit. He already enjoyed a national reputation for toughness, balanced with an uncompromising dedication to justice. If his terms were harsh, the delegation was, nonetheless, willing, to concede to them. Accordingly, on January 12, 1921, the club owners of both leagues ratified his election as Commissioner of Baseball for a seven-year term at a salary of $50,000. He was to be reelected to this post three times and he remained undisputed czar of baseball until his death at seventy-eight on November 25, 1944.

His flowing white hair, heavily pouched eyes, and weathered hawklike face were to become as familiar to baseball fans as the faces of the greatest stars. Besides his picturesque appearance and caustic wit, he had a will that was as immovable as the bit of Georgia for which he was named. He was completely uncompromising in applying the letter of the law to wealthy club owners and second-string players alike.

In his first year in office, Judge Landis demonstrated his readiness to tangle with anyone who stepped out of line or failed to live completely within the framework of baseball laws. The first to test the strength of the diminutive judge was none other than the Sultan of Swat himself—Babe Ruth.

On January 12, 1921, the club owners of both leagues ratified the election of Judge Kennesaw Mountain Landis (opposite) as Commissioner of Baseball. Landis was a man of strong, unimpeachable character, who could command respect and restore public faith in baseball after the Black Sox Scandal. His flowing white hair, heavily pouched eyes, and weathered hawklike face were to become as familiar to baseball fans as the faces of the greatest stars.

The House that Ruth Built

Babe Ruth's run-in with Judge Landis did not come until the end of the 1921 season—the season that marked the first time in history that the New York Yankees won a pennant. It was also the first season that Babe Ruth began to smash systematically just about every existing batting record in baseball.

Almost as if to prove his fifty-four home-run record of the previous year was no fluke, Babe rapped a total of fifty-nine during the 1921 season. He also brought his batting average up to .378, scored 177 runs, and drove in 170 runs. Opposing ball clubs were frantic trying to devise some sort of defense against Babe. There's not much a team can do against a ball that goes sailing out of the park, but Ruth also belted forty-four doubles and sixteen triples that year—almost all of them hit to right field. Some teams began having their outfields shift to the right whenever Babe came to bat and some even had the second baseman move out a bit into right field. To counter this strategy, Ruth punched a few past the pitcher, to where the second baseman should have been, and soon that man was back where he belonged. Babe didn't bunt very often, but every now and then he would upset the applecart and lay down a bunt that usually caught the infielders napping. Pitchers soon found that the safest thing to do was to give Babe an intentional base on balls whenever possible. This in itself led to another of the Babe's records that still stands in the record books. During his career, Ruth was given a total of 2056 bases on balls—many of them intentional.

The pennant race of 1921 was a two-team affair all the way. The Cleveland Indians were the 1920 champions and, managed by Babe's old friend Tris Speaker, defended their championship right down to the wire. The Yankees were host to the Indians in the Polo Grounds very near the end of the season with the two teams virtually tied for first place. The team that could take three out of the four games in the series would be almost assured of the pennant. With two wins and a loss going into the final game, the Yankees badly needed a victory. They got it in one of the wildest games of the season. Babe Ruth whacked two homers and a double, driving in four runs to lead the Yankees to an 8–7 victory. A few days later the Yankees clinched the pennant in the American League as did the New York Giants in the National League. It would be an all-New York World Series.

The Yankees started the series in great fashion, winning the first two games by the identical scores of 3–0. In the third game they scored four more runs before the Giants even got their first run of the series. But victory for the Yankees was not in the cards that year and they lost the series five games to three.

For the Babe it was heartbreak as he was forced to sit on the bench for the last three games. In the first five games he did all that was expected of him as he hit his first World Series home run and batted in four runs while averaging .313 at the plate. But he developed an ugly abscess on his left elbow which soon became so painful he could no longer play.

A sportswriter who evidently did not know the Babe lived for only one thing —to play baseball—accused him of being a slacker. In his column the writer referred to Ruth's "alleged injury" and implied that Babe was happy to have the pressure of World Series play off him. As the Babe recalled later, "I blew my top and decided to show him my arm. The lancing job on it had left some of the bone exposed. I went after him."

"You're accusing me of not having any guts." Babe yelled at the terrified writer. "Now, if *you* have any, print a picture of my arm with this hole in it and let your readers see my side of it." The picture was never printed but Babe had made his point to everyone in the press box. No one would ever again imply that the Babe was a slacker.

The clash with Judge Landis came soon after the World Series ended. The commissioner had put through a rule which prohibited players on pennant-winning teams from barnstorming after the World Series. Post-season exhibition games on a barnstorming tour were a lucrative enterprise in those days, and millions of fans around the country

would flock to see the great Babe Ruth in action. Babe and two other Yankees, Bob Meusel and Bill Piercy, decided to go ahead with a post-season tour anyway, despite Landis' personal admonition that there would be "a lot of consequences."

Babe's abscessed elbow was soon healed and the pick-up team he had assembled began their tour in upper New York State. The Yankee management could see, even if Ruth couldn't, that Judge Landis meant business and Colonel Houston tried to get Babe and his pals back in Landis' good graces. It didn't work.

On December 5, Landis made his ruling. It read in part, "The situation involves not merely rule violation but, rather, a mutinous defiance by the players intended to present the question; Which is the bigger, baseball or any individual in baseball?"

"There will be an order forfeiting their share of the World Series funds and suspending them until May 20, 1922, on which date, and within ten days thereafter, they will be eligible to apply for reinstatement."

Pressure from all quarters was immediately brought to bear on the judge in an effort to get him to relent on his decision. But as the Babe said, "The old judge was about as easy to budge as an alp." The Yankee management pleaded with Landis. With Ruth out of the lineup, attendance was bound to drop and that would cost the club money. By this time Ed Barrow, Babe's old Red Sox manager, had been hired by the Yankees as general manager and Colonels Houston and Ruppert sent Ed to see the judge in person. But Landis put Barrow on the spot with the question, "Just what would you have done if you were in my place?" Barrow shuffled his feet uncomfortably and said, "I would have done exactly as you did, Judge." And that was the end of that.

The judge's decision cost the players exactly $3,362.26 plus a month's pay. The greatest agony of all for Babe, though, was sitting out the first thirty-nine days of the 1922 season. But the question of which was bigger, the game or the individual, had been answered

with finality. After watching the greatest of them all meet an unhappy fate, no other player ever disputed the word of the Commissioner of Baseball. And neither did Babe Ruth.

The Babe never really reached peak form in 1922. In the home run department he managed only thirty-five, while Ken Williams of the Browns knocked in thirty-nine to beat out Babe for the first time in five years. Ruth's batting average also dropped to .315— still a respectable average in any league, though certainly not what was expected of the Babe. But the Yankees won the pennant anyway and, for the second year in a row, faced the Giants in an all-New York World Series.

The series ended in complete humiliation for the Yankees. They didn't win a game. They had at least one good excuse for their dismal showing, however. Babe Ruth turned in one of the most disappointing performances of his career. He got only two hits, a single and a double, in seventeen times at bat for a dismal average of .118. The Babe felt miserable about this showing. The games all had been close and a hit or two by the Babe might have made the difference. Referring to the close scores Babe said, "It is easy to see how my failure to hit let down my ball club."

But, characteristically, the penitent Babe never offered excuses or alibis for his playing. "People have asked me," he wrote later, "how a hitter of my reputation and ability could have gone through a five-game series with such a punk showing. My reply is that it was just one of those things that can happen to a regular as easily as it can happen to a sub."

The statement also demonstrates another characteristic of Babe Ruth. He might have said "those things can happen to a star." It wasn't false modesty that caused him to choose the word "regular." For the Babe, being a regular on a championship baseball team was about all the honor a player should expect. His greatest pride was to earn a starting position in the New York Yankee lineup—and there were eight other fellows with the same qualifications.

Babe had a way of bouncing back from a bad season or a bad series, and as 1922 drew to a close he looked forward to 1923 with renewed determina-

tion. Writing about this period many years later he said, "Looking back at my career and my numerous mistakes, I think I usually had good intentions. In some respects that .118 batting average in the 1922 World Series may have been a very good thing for me. I knew I let down my teammates, also the fans; and I also thought of the kids all over the country who had been watching my play in that series. As I started training for the 1923 season I decided I wasn't going to let those youngsters down again. I was beginning to develop some kind of a sense of duty to the kids."

True to his word, the Babe turned in one of the greatest season performances of his career in 1923—the first to be played in the brand-new Yankee Sta-

dium. That famed baseball park is often referred to as "The House That Ruth Built." With new attendance records being set as the fans poured through the gates to see the Babe hit home runs, the Yankees could afford a stadium of their own. It was the greatest ball park ever built up to that day.

The stadium was opened on April 18, 1923, and some 75,000 fans turned out to overflow the park which had a seating capacity of only 65,000. It was a great occasion and the mayor of New York was there along with Judge Landis and many other dignitaries. It was a great day for the Yankees as they beat the Red Sox by a score of 4–1. And it was a great day for Babe Ruth as he whacked a homer into the right-field bleachers in the fourth inning.

"I hit a few more in there during the next twelve years I played there," the Babe wrote later. "Kids will be hitting them there when I'm gone, but I'm kind of glad I hit the first one."

The Yankees romped home with the American League pennant that year fourteen games ahead of the second-place team. And Babe Ruth turned in the highest batting average of his career—.393—along with forty-one homers, forty-five doubles, and thirteen triples. The results lent credence to the saying then going around, "As Ruth goes, so go the Yankees."

In the World Series that year, the Yankees once again met their old enemies from across the Harlem River —the Giants. This time, though, things were different. The Yankees walloped the Giants, four games to two and won their first world championship.

And Babe Ruth didn't let down his fans, his teammates, or the "kids" as he had in 1922. This time he belted three home runs and logged a handsome .368 batting average. The Babe was back in form once more.

Yankee Stadium—The House That Ruth Built—was opened in 1923. The Yankees romped home with the American League pennant that year and Babe Ruth (left) turned in a .393 batting average, the highest of his career.

The year 1923 was also a milestone in the history of the Yankees. In June a big first baseman by the name of Lou Gehrig joined the team. In later years he and the Babe were to become the greatest one-two punch in the history of baseball.

In the 1924 season the Yankees and the Babe played beautiful ball. But while they fought tooth and nail with Ty Cobb's Detroit Tigers, the Washington Senators came out of nowhere to capture the pennant by a scant two and a half games.

The 1925 season was a disaster for both the Yankees and Babe Ruth. "I changed from batting champion in 1924 to the big bust of 1925," the Babe said ruefully. "My batting average caved in to .290. . . . I hit only twenty-five homers and Bob Meusel dethroned me as home-run king."

Just before the opening of the season Babe was taken ill, seriously ill, and collapsed in the train station at Asheville, North Carolina. This episode in Ruth's life later became known as "the tummyache heard around the world," but it was very nearly the end of Babe Ruth. After weeks of convalescing, first in Asheville and then in New York, the Babe finally returned to the team in May. But he never got back in the groove during that 1925 season.

He did, however, get in trouble with Manager Miller Huggins. The episode ended in a showdown that made newspaper headlines across the country. Babe had taken to devoting more and more time to his night life and began showing up late at the ball park. Finally Huggins had taken all he could of this sort of behavior and one day told Ruth,

"This time you've gone too far. You're suspended indefinitely, and I've got some more news for you—you're fined $5000."

"You can't do this to me," the Babe yelled. "I'll go to New York and see Ruppert." By this time Colonel Ruppert was the sole owner of the Yankees, having bought out Houston's share in 1923. Both Ruppert and general manager Ed Barrow backed Huggins all the way and when Babe got back to New York he discovered that "maybe I did overrate my place in the Yankee organization." As Babe wrote in later years, "I was quickly given to understand that Huggins was boss of the ball club and that I was just another player. What's more, I was told my suspension would last until such time as Huggins lifted it."

When the team returned to New York, Babe apologized to the little manager who soon put the now-wiser Ruth back in the lineup. "I'm not proud of this chapter of my baseball life," Babe said later. "It is one of those things a man would like to change if he could alter the past. But men and boys learn from experience, and I believe I learned something from this one. I knew that although Huggins was a little man in stature, he was the boss, and I had acted like a spoiled child."

And so the roller-coaster career of Babe Ruth had hit another dip, but he was now prepared for the long ascent to another and perhaps more significant peak. This was the era of the "Roaring Twenties," a golden age filled with colorful and flamboyant characters who left their mark for good or bad on the pages of history. In boxing, the great Jack Dempsey ruled the heavyweights and

Bobby Jones was setting new records on golf links around the nation. It was the jazz age and the day of the "flappers." It was the day of the silent screen when Rudolph Valentino set hearts throbbing in movie houses around the world and a little clown named Charlie Chaplin reduced audiences to tears of laughter.

Across the sea in Germany an ex-corporal by the name of Adolf Hitler was languishing in jail and writing a book called *Mein Kampf*. In Italy a strutting little man named Benito Mussolini had gradually assumed dictatorial powers under the banner of Fascism.

But in America they were reading books written by F. Scott Fitzgerald, Sinclair Lewis, and Ernest Hemingway. Americans in "Tin Lizzies" and raccoon coats lived, loved, and laughed under a banner of peace and record prosperity. It was a nation in search of thrills and adventure and the people thrived on the exploits of such men as Charles Lindbergh, Commander Richard E. Byrd, and racing-car driver Barney Oldfield. The American public adored their heroes, especially if they were colorful and exciting. For that reason, Babe Ruth was the most-beloved sports figure of the decade.

In June of 1923, a big first baseman by the name of Lou Gehrig (left) joined the Yankees. In later years he and the Babe were to become the greatest one-two punch in the history of baseball.

"Hello, Babe Ruth speaking," said the Sultan of Swat as he answered the telephone at Yankee Stadium. It was the day before the opening game of the 1926 World Series between the Yankees and the St. Louis Cardinals.

"Mr. Ruth," said the voice on the telephone, "this is Mr. Sylvester out in Essex Falls, New Jersey, and I would like to ask a favor of you. I have a sick boy, ten years old, who has been through an operation that the doctors say was successful, but," and his voice choked up, "but Johnny seems to have lost the will to live."

Babe Ruth was immediately full of sympathy on hearing news that a boy was sick. "Kids" were a special interest of his and any time he could lend inspiration to a boy he was ready.

"I wonder," continued the man, "if you could please send Johnny a letter or, even better, an autographed baseball? You are his hero and I'm sure a memento from you would help a lot."

"Where is Essex Falls?" asked the Babe. The man told him and Ruth said, "I'll be out to see him personally this afternoon." Even with the World Series starting on the following day, Babe would not fail to heed a call for help from a "kid." He immediately left for Essex Falls.

No one told Johnny that Babe Ruth was coming. His doctors felt that a strong emotional jolt would be just the stimulant the boy needed. The boy's eyes popped as through the door of his bedroom came the one and only Babe Ruth.

Babe sat on the edge of Johnny's bed and talked about baseball. He had brought an autographed ball, a glove, and a bat for Johnny, and he told the boy he expected he'd soon be well enough to use them. As Johnny gradually overcame his initial shock, he began to brighten perceptibly. Soon he was showing an interest and spirit that had been missing since his operation. The doctor smiled as he watched the results of the Babe Ruth therapy.

Johnny's parents, standing behind the Babe, fought back tears of joy as their boy began to perk up.

Johnny had one last request as the Babe was leaving. "Will you hit a home run for me in the World Series, Mr. Ruth?"

Babe smiled. "Sure Keed," he said, "tomorrow afternoon."

Then he rubbed Johnny's head for luck and headed back for New York to prepare for the opening game.

As it turned out, Babe hit four home runs in that 1926 World Series and, with each one, Johnny gained new strength. They were "his" home runs and the one and only Babe Ruth was hitting them just for Johnny Sylvester.

Johnny did get well and subsequently went on to college at Princeton and became a naval officer during World War II. Then one day in April, 1947, Johnny Sylvester—now thirty years old—repaid the visit. Not long after the Babe had left the hospital, still gravely ill, Johnny came to try to bolster the spirits of the great man who had once inspired him to get well.

The two had a long friendly chat in Babe's apartment and the old ballplayer was deeply moved by the visit. In all his baseball career, Babe Ruth had never turned down a request to visit with children. Now, in his time of need, one had returned to repay a gesture of good will. This visit with Johnny was a great thrill for Ruth. You see, in 1926—just for the Babe—Johnny had taken a new, powerful swing at life. In a sense, he had hit a home run for Babe Ruth.

The Greatest
Baseball Team
of All Time

The Yankees won the American League pennant once again in 1926, startling the baseball world as they came back in championship style after their seventh-place finish the previous year. And the Babe bounced back also to spark the team with forty-eight home runs and a batting average of .372.

Manager Huggins was genuinely pleased with Babe's performance both on and off the playing field. "Babe," he told the big fellow, "I admire a man who can win over a lot of tough opponents, but I admire even more a man who can win over himself." The compliment pleased Ruth, but Huggins still would not rescind the $5000 fine he had placed on Babe during the previous year.

The Yankees met the St. Louis Cardinals in the World Series. Playing for the Cards that season were two of baseball's greatest—Grover Cleveland Alexander and Rogers Hornsby. Each now share a niche in baseball's Hall of Fame along with Babe Ruth.

The series went the full distance of seven games before the outcome was decided—and the Cards won it four games to three. Alexander, a grand old man of forty with twenty years of pitching behind him, wrapped the series up for St. Louis. After winning the sixth game he returned the very next day to pitch two and one-third innings in relief and saved the final game for the Cards' starter Jesse Haines.

The Babe also had a great series and set a new record by blasting three home runs in one game at Sportsmans Park in St. Louis. The first two went clean over the roof of the pavilion and the third didn't stop until it hit the wall of the Y.M.C.A. building across the street from the park. Once again, the fans went away shaking their heads in awe at the almost unbelievable hitting power of Babe Ruth.

And so, as the 1926 baseball season ended, the stage was set for the Babe's greatest year of his entire career—the season of 1927.

Whenever baseball writers or old-time ballplayers get together, the talk invariably gets around to the question of "which was the greatest baseball team of all time?" Like the issue of whether Joe Louis or Jack Dempsey was the better fighter, the answer will never be found or proven. There are millions of fans, however, who are convinced that their choice is the right and logical one. There is one contention, however, that receives the unreserved support of many baseball authorities including Babe Ruth—that the 1927 New York Yankees were the greatest baseball team in history.

In a poll taken by *The Sporting News* of 140 members of the Baseball Writer's Association, in which the question of the greatest team was posed, the Yankees of 1927 received a total of seventy-one votes. The most votes received by any other team was fifteen for the Chicago White Sox of 1919.

As for the Babe, he put it this way: "A man who had put away his baseball togs after an eventful life in the game must live on his memories, some good, some bad. Of the good ones the one that stands out the most of all is that of the greatest ball club that ever stepped onto a field . . . the 1927 Yankees."

A few figures will serve to demonstrate the Yankees' superiority over the other teams in the league that year: They scored nearly 1000 runs, won 110 games while losing only 44, belted 158 homers, and beat out the second-place Athletics by 19 games. Five members of the starting lineup had batting averages of over .300 and they had four pitchers who won 18 or more games during the season. There are numerous other figures that Yankee backers use to measure the greatness of the 1927 team. But another indication of how they dominated the league lies in the fact that during the season they beat the St. Louis Browns twenty-one consecutive times.

For Babe Ruth, the year 1927 marked the high point of his baseball career. In that season he hit sixty home runs—more than any rival club in the league hit as a team. In addition he batted a handsome .356, scored 158 runs, and drove in 164. He also received the Most Valuable Player award.

Perhaps the biggest factor behind Babe's sixty home runs was the fact that Lou Gehrig was moved up to fourth in the batting order in 1927—just behind Ruth. As the Babe later told it, "I don't think I ever would have established my home-run record of sixty if it hadn't been for Lou . . . Pitchers began pitching to me, because if they passed me they still had Lou to contend with." And pitching to Gehrig could be almost as dangerous as pitching to Ruth—big Lou hit forty-seven home runs that year himself.

Ever since that season of 1927, whenever a ballplayer begins to hit home runs with regularity, fans and writers compare his pace with that of Babe Ruth's record. Many have kept up the pace until near the end of the season—but Babe hit seventeen in September—a pretty tough hurdle to make. No other man has made it yet. Another Yankee of a later day, Roger Maris, hit 61 home runs in the 162-game season of 1961. But Babe's record still stands for a 154-game season.

The World Series of 1927 found the Yankees tangling with the Pittsburgh Pirates. It is often said that the Yankees won that series before it even started.

One day before the opening game, the Pirates finished listening to a pep talk by their manager about the time the Yankees began taking batting practice. The Pirates had never seen the American League champs so they stayed around to watch the workout. As the Babe told it later, "We really put on a show. Lou and I banged ball after ball into the right-field stands, and I finally knocked one out of the park in right center. Bob Meusel and Tony Lazzeri kept hammering balls into the left-field seats." As writer Tom Meany tells it, "The Yanks put on one of the most awesome exhibitions of slugging ever seen. ...while the Pirates sat in open-mouthed wonder. There are those who maintain that just by looking at the batting drill of the Yankees, the Pirates lost all hope."

Whatever the reason, the results are in the record books. The Yankees clubbed the hopeless Pirates into the dust in four straight games. Babe Ruth got six hits, two of them homers, and scored four runs as his contribution to the one-sided affair.

The season and World Series of 1927 can be said to be the high-water mark of Babe Ruth's career. There would be other great days, fine seasons, and new records set or old ones broken. But the tide now began to ebb for the Yankees and for the Babe. There would never be another team so perfectly tuned, so finely balanced as the Yanks of 1927.

The Yankees won the pennant again in 1928, though this time by a bare two games over the Philadelphia Athletics, the team they had left so far behind in 1927. The series that year was played against the St. Louis Cardinals, who had edged the Yankees in 1926. This time, though, it was a different story as the Yankees humiliated them in four straight games. The Yankees had now

For Babe Ruth, the year 1927 marked the high point of his baseball career. This was the season in which he hit sixty home runs—more than any rival club in the league hit as a team. One of the big factors behind Babe's sixty home runs was the fact that Lou Gehrig was moved up to fourth in the batting order—just behind Ruth. Pitching to Gehrig could be almost as dangerous as pitching to Ruth—Lou hit forty-seven home runs that year. Opposite, Gehrig shakes hands as Ruth crosses the plate after a home run.

won two straight World Series without the loss of a single game.

The Babe set a new record in the series also as he got nine hits for sixteen times at bat and a fantastic .625 average. And once again he pulled the incredible feat of belting three successive home runs just as he had in the same park in 1926.

In his autobiography, Babe tells of another facet of his career that would always give him pride and satisfaction. "My interest in kids kept sharpening," he wrote, "until I reached the point where I got as much kick out of my association with them as they seemed to receive from their meetings with me."

He recalled an incident in the spring of 1928 when a man approached him in a hotel lobby in Knoxville. "He had been crying," Babe remembered, "and begged me to drive with him to his cabin—somewhere out in the hills—where he had a sick son." As it turned out, the exhibition game scheduled for that day was called off because of rain and Babe went with the fellow.

"It took all day to get to the cabin and back to town," Babe wrote, "but the look on that kid's pale, sick face was enough of a reward for me."

And Babe could never forget "St. Mary's, Brother Matthias, and the kids I left behind in Baltimore. I kept going back. Most of the boys I knew had left, the great majority of them to become useful citizens in the outside world. But other kids slept in our old beds, worked at our old benches, played in the same yard and my heart was with them." Babe once took the school band on a tour with the Yankees where they played concerts for the fans. The public responded generously and their contributions went toward replacing some of the school's buildings that had burned down.

In January of 1929, Babe's wife Helen burned to death when a fire consumed their farm in Massachusetts. The couple had not been together for several years, but true to his Catholic faith Babe could never seek a divorce. They had started adoption proceedings on a little girl named Dorothy and, thankfully, she was spared Helen's fate. Babe had to report for spring training right after the funeral and he was very much concerned about seven-year-old Dorothy. But on opening day of the 1929 baseball season Babe took a step that was to change both his and Dorothy's life. At five o'clock on the morning of April 17, 1929, Babe remarried.

Babe had met Claire Merritt Hodgson in Washington, D.C., at a game in Griffith Stadium. "Claire had many things I did not possess," Babe wrote later. "Culture, background, good looks. She was born in Jefferson, Georgia, but grew up in Athens, where her father, James Monroe Merritt, taught law at the University of Georgia. Claire chose a career on the stage."

Claire was a widow. She had a little girl named Julia who was eleven at the time. Soon after the wedding Babe formally adopted both Julia and Dorothy. Claire and his newly acquired family wrought a significant change in the personal habits of the Babe. Claire was to exert a steadying influence on the Babe for the rest of his days. She was, he said, "a faithful wife, friend, counselor, and pal." As for Claire, she was to write later: "The Babe and I never fell out of love, not even for a minute."

And so the year 1929, which began with a tragedy, was marked in April by one of the happiest and most significant moments of his life. The baseball season proved a disappointment as the Yankees finished second to the Athletics who won their first pennant in fifteen years. Then tragedy struck once again. On September 25, the Yankee's manager, little Miller Huggins, suddenly passed away. The Babe was stunned by the loss, as were the other members of the team. Most of them had been involved in clashes with the fiery little manager—Ruth more than any of them. But they all respected his knowledge of the game and they knew they would miss "Hug" in the coming season. The funeral was at the Little Church Around the Corner, in downtown Manhattan and the Babe "knelt there and cried when the minister spoke his last words."

A month later came the great stock market "crash" which marked the end of the unparalleled prosperity of the twenties and the beginning of the great

Babe Ruth and his second wife, Claire Merritt Hodgson (right), as they appeared shortly before their marriage on April 17, 1929.

depression of the thirties. For Babe Ruth it had been an eventful year.

The year 1930 saw the Yankees, now under the management of Bob Shawkey, slip to third place. But Babe, despite the depression, signed a contract for $80,000—the highest, up to that time, in the history of baseball. His salary was now greater than that of the president of the United States.

When Shawkey was released as manager at the end of the 1930 season, Babe had great hopes of getting the job. Many of his teammates, fans, and baseball writers felt he was the man for the position. But all his past indiscretions and wild living were firmly implanted in the minds of Ed Barrow and Colonel Ruppert. "You can't manage yourself, how do expect to manage others?" was Ruppert's philosophy. The new manager named was Joe McCarthy, who would become a legend himself during his great career with the Yankees.

McCarthy, with a great assist from Babe Ruth and Lou Gehrig, brought the Yankees up to second place in 1931 and in 1932 piloted the club back to first place. The World Series that year was played against the Chicago Cubs and the Yankees did it again—they took the series in four straight games.

For the first time, Lou Gehrig outshone the Babe in World Series competition. While Babe got two homers and averaged .333, Lou averaged .529 and belted three round-trippers. It was a big year for Lou all the way, with his series performance the crowning achievement. Babe would always say that one of his greatest thrills was watching Lou drive four home runs in one game on June 3 of that year. It is a record unexcelled to this day.

The season of 1933 was the last in which Babe Ruth averaged over .300 or knocked in more than thirty home runs, as the Yankees once again fell to second place. This was also the year of the first All-Star game and Babe had the honor of belting the first home run in All-Star competition as the American Leaguers downed the Nationals by a score of 4–2.

In 1934 Babe's batting average plummeted to .288 and he managed only twenty-two home runs—certainly re-

Soon after Babe and Claire were married, he formally adopted Julia, the eleven-year-old daughter of Claire's first marriage and Dorothy, a seven-year-old ward of Babe and his first wife. Opposite, top: Babe (at desk) signs the adoption papers as (left to right) Claire, Dorothy, and Julia look on. Opposite, bottom: Babe signs a New York Yankees contract in 1930 for a salary of $80,000—the highest, up to that time, in the history of baseball. Looking on is Colonel Jacob Ruppert, owner of the Yankees.

It was an angry Babe Ruth who came to bat in the fifth inning of the third game of the 1932 World Series. The partisan Chicago crowd at Wrigley Field had made Babe a special target of their abuse and antipathy. Many Cub rooters had even brought fruit and vegetables with which to pelt the invading Yankees. After four innings, Babe's left-field position was littered with everything from lemons to tomatoes.

The rivalry between New York and Chicago teams was traditional, and this series was no exception. The first two games, played in Yankee Stadium, had gone to the power-laden Yankees by scores of 12-6 and 5-2. Now, in this homecoming game in Chicago, Wrigley Field was charged with tension.

Babe was doing his best to restrain his anger. He would not give the crowd the satisfaction of knowing they had succeeded in riling him. But Cub catcher Gabby Hartnett knew. And umpire Roy Van Graflan knew. They could see the fury burning in Ruth's eyes. They could see the knuckles whiten as Babe gripped his bat with grim intensity.

As he dug his spikes into the dirt of the batter's box, Babe glowered menacingly at the Chicago pitcher. But Charley Root was undismayed. Picking up his catcher's signal, Root checked the runner at first base and then turned and fired the first pitch straight down the middle for a called strike.

As Van Graflan called "Strike one!" Babe stepped back a pace and raised one index finger for the crowd to see. "Strike one!" he bellowed, as if to verify the umpire's call. With this, the fans increased their hooting and razzing. The Cub second-stringers on the bench came out on the steps of their dugout to lend vocal assistance to the crowd.

Charley Root went into his windup once again and blazed another strike across the plate as Babe took it with his bat on his shoulder. "Strike two!" roared the Babe, holding up two fingers for the crowd to see. The jeering howls from the stands raised to a crescendo and the Cubs on the dugout steps thumbed their noses and danced with glee.

Then came one of the most thrilling and dramatic moments in the history of base-ball. As Root prepared for his third pitch, Babe turned with monumental contempt to the Cubs dugout and then pointed with his bat toward the flagpole in center field. There could be no doubt of his meaning. He intended to hit a home run. Furthermore, he intended that ball to go into the center-field bleachers — the farthermost point in the park. The crowd blinked its disbelief and then roared derision.

Never in the history of the game had anyone, especially a veteran star, voluntarily put himself into such a potentially embarrassing situation. If he struck out now— and he had only one strike left—Babe would never live it down. He would take a jeering in every game he ever played for the rest of his life. But the gesture had been made, and Root threw the final pitch.

Baseball strategists will always maintain that Root should have wasted a pitch— that is, purposely thrown a ball in hopes of getting the angry Babe to go for a bad one. But Root, too, was in a disdainful mood and the pitch he threw was a fast ball, right around the knees. The Babe stepped into it and his massive arms and shoulders swished that big bat with all the pent-up fury in his gigantic frame. The powerful wrists snapped with perfect timing and bat met ball with a resounding whack. A stunned silence fell over the crowd and the Cub dugout as a hundred-thousand eyes watched the ball rifle straight for the target—the flagpole in center field. In a long, hush-filled moment, it disappeared into the center-field bleachers.

As Babe trotted happily around the bases, the scowl was gone and he grinned from ear to ear. As he turned past second base, the silence was suddenly broken as the crowd began to cheer. The basic good sportsmanship and better nature of the fans overcame their partisan emotions. The spontaneous ovation increased to a thundering roar as the Babe crossed home plate. The fans were paying tribute to a tremendous performance by the greatest showman in the game. Even the Cubs, who moments before had been jeering the Babe, took off their caps in a salute to the Sultan of Swat.

It was bravado at its boldest and it has happened only once. But then—there was only one Babe Ruth.

spectable figures in any league. But not what the fans expected of Babe Ruth or what he expected of himself. At the end of the season he and Claire, along with the Lou Gehrigs and the Lefty Gomezes, went off on an exhibition tour of Japan, Shanghai, and Manila, returning home by way of Suez, France, and England.

When Babe arrived home he found his 1935 contract waiting for him. Baseball law required that a contract be forwarded prior to January 1 of the contract year. His salary had been $35,000 for the 1934 season. The new contract called for one dollar. Babe's days as a Yankee were over.

The contract, of course, was supposed to be an interim arrangement while Babe proved himself in spring training. The Yankee management would watch closely how the Babe performed, and before the start of the regular season presumably would offer him a contract for what they deemed him worth. In the meantime, the Yankees offered Babe a job as manager of their Newark minor-league club, but Babe turned it down. He had his pride and he was a big leaguer. He wanted to manage a major-league team. "I don't think I was talking out of turn," he wrote later. "I just felt I had the same right to start a managerial career in the majors as Cobb, Speaker, Hornsby, Sisler, Cochrane, Harris, Cronin, and others had been given."

About this time the Boston Braves offered Babe a position as vice president, assistant manager, and right fielder for the 1935 season at a salary of $35,000.

Babe took the offer; it was probably the only time in baseball history that a vice president played in right field. The offer sounded good, but it soon became apparent that the Braves wanted Babe only for the number of fans his name would bring through the turnstiles. There was friction and mutual dissatisfaction right from the start.

Babe reported for spring training with the Braves at St. Petersburg and "for the first time in my life, baseball was a drudgery." As he wrote later, "It was more and more of an effort to move over the outfield or run down to first base. I was forty-one and playing my twenty-second season in the big leagues . . . kids were striking me out or making me pop up on balls I could have hit out of the lot a few years before. It was a rotten feeling."

Of the season, Babe was to say, "It was pretty much of a nightmare. If I had it to do over again, the last 28 games of my 2053 and my last six home runs would never have been entered into the records."

Babe Ruth played his final game on May 30, 1935, in Philadelphia against the Phillies. "I played only a few innings and then retired for the day, with a charley horse," the Babe would remember. "It was the last time my name appeared in a major-league box score."

On June 2, Babe called the baseball writers to the dressing room at Braves Field in Boston. When they were assembled, Babe announced, "I'm quitting," as simply as that. The active playing career of the greatest player the game had ever seen was over.

In 1935, the Boston Braves hired Babe as vice- president, assistant manager, and right fielder. Here he is shown at Braves' spring training camp in St. Petersburg, Florida, as he autographs baseballs for a group of children.

No Help Wanted

"I wanted to stay in baseball more than I ever wanted anything in my life," Babe wrote later. "But in 1935 there was no job for me, and that embittered me.

"I felt completely lost at first. I thought I'd wake up and find it was a bad dream, and when it became apparent that it wasn't a dream I felt certain that the phone would ring and it would be the Yankees or some other big league-team in search of me—telling me it was all a mistake. But the phone didn't ring."

Claire would always remember those agonizing days that stretched into months and then years following Babe's retirement. "I know no words for his despondency," she wrote. "He kept himself busy with his hunting and fish-ing and golf. Whenever he entered the house there was always the same un-spoken question plastered all over his big, tanned face, 'Any phone calls?' . . . usually there was only a helpless shrug filled with bewilderment and pain. And now and then there were hot tears of frustration."

Babe was not in need of money. Baseball had made him a wealthy man. Thanks principally to his business man-ager, Christy Walsh, Babe's annuities were paying him fine dividends now that his playing days were behind him. There were also personal appearances, radio shows, and endorsements of all kinds which made his retirement years among the most lucrative of his life. But Babe's big heart ached to be back in the big leagues.

Finally, in 1938, about mid-way through the baseball season, the long-awaited phone call came. It was from Larry MacPhail, then general manager of the Brooklyn Dodgers, and he offered Babe a coaching job. Babe was ecstatic and he accepted without a moment's hesitation. The Dodgers finished in seventh place that year, but Babe enjoyed "working with those kids in the hitting cage." In addition to coaching, Babe played in ten exhibition games which were quickly scheduled after he was hired. Fans poured through the gates to see the old "Sultan of Swat," and the exhibition games grossed some $14,000—almost enough to pay Babe's salary for the whole period he was with the club. But disappointment came once again as Leo Durocher was named man-ager beginning with the 1939 season. Leo and Babe never did get along and Babe said: "I knew I wouldn't return to the Dodgers."

The year 1939 marked one of the saddest occasions of Babe's life. His old friend and Yankee teammate, Lou Gehrig, the "Iron Horse" who had played in 2130 consecutive games, was seriously ill. Following a checkup at the Mayo Clinic the world was informed that Lou was dying. He had played his last game for the Yankees in June, and on July 4 they staged a "Lou Gehrig Day" at Yankee Stadium. Babe and a lot of the other old-time Yankees turned up to pay tribute to their long-time friend and teammate.

One by one various dignitaries spoke kind words of Lou, and then Lou him-

self took over the microphone. As Babe remembered it, "Lou spoke as I never thought I'd hear a man speak in a ball park. Every word he said plainly came from his heart and the big crowd of more than 60,000 sat there in the stands and there wasn't a dry eye anywhere. He spoke of Mom and Pop Gehrig, and Eleanor, his wife, and what the Yanks had meant to him, and when he said, 'I consider myself the luckiest man in the world,' I couldn't stand it any longer.

"I went over to him and put my arm around him, and though I tried to smile and cheer him up, I could not keep from crying."

Lou died on June 2, 1941.

Though no one could suspect it on that Lou Gehrig Day in 1939, it would be only nine years later that the other half of the most famous twosome in baseball history would be standing at the same home plate under very similar conditions.

In December of 1941, the Japanese struck Pearl Harbor and America found itself plunged into war. In August of the following year Babe was asked to put on a hitting exhibition before a game being played for Army-Navy Relief. The Babe, of course, jumped at the chance to don once again the old Yankee uniform and swing a bat in "The House That Ruth Built."

To pitch balls to the Babe, the Yankees brought in the incomparable "Big Train" Walter Johnson. Babe had not swung a bat in four years and Johnson hadn't pitched a ball in many years. But both were willing to do their part for the armed services.

Some 60,000 fans screamed a welcome to the all-time greats and Johnson pitched a few warm-up pitches to Benny Bengough, the old New York catcher. Finally Johnson seemed to find the groove and the Babe stepped into the batter's box. The fans settled back to wait for a home run. Johnson threw twenty-one pitches, some of which Babe hit into the lower stands, before Ruth finally connected with the ball as in the old days. It was a hit of true "Ruthian" proportions and it climbed higher and higher into the bright blue sky before landing in the third deck of the stadium in right field. Babe tossed his bat aside and trotted with that old familiar pigeon-toed gait around the bases. Johnson was there to meet Babe as he crossed the plate, and the two delighted old-timers trotted off the field to a thunderous applause. Sixty-thousand fans could now boast, along with millions of older fans, that they, too, had seen the Babe clobber one.

Throughout the war, Babe helped sell war bonds and wherever he appeared was always a hit with the servicemen. The same soldiers, sailors, and marines who crowded around the Babe during that period had thronged around the same man when they were children and he was the "Sultan of Swat." Babe's "kids" had grown up and were busy in the deadly game of striking out the Axis.

On Guadalcanal, the Japanese, many of whom spoke English, resorted to unusual tactics in their battle with the United States Marines. Thousands of them had seen the Babe play in pre-war exhibition games in Japan and thousands more had read about him. They assumed he must be a national hero in the United States and they began screaming derogatory remarks about Babe Ruth in an effort to provoke the Marines into giving away their positions. Happily, the ruse proved ineffectual, but it does serve to demonstrate the impression Babe and his home runs made on the Japanese.

On more than one occasion in the European theater, American units used the challenge word "Yankees" for which

In 1939, Lou Gehrig—Babe's old friend and Yankee teammate—became seriously ill. On July 4, the Yankees staged a "Lou Gehrig Day" at Yankee Stadium. Babe and other old-time Yankees came to pay tribute to the "Iron Horse." When Lou had finished speaking that day, Babe went over and put his arm around him (opposite). As Babe said later, "though I tried to smile and cheer him up, I could not keep from crying."

the answering password was "Ruth." Any red-blooded American youth would immediately recognize the relationship between the two words which were as natural a combination and as typically American as ham and eggs. But the relationship was alien to a foreign mind.

Late in 1946, a number of persons close to the Babe began to comment about the hoarseness of his voice. At the same time he began suffering from severe head pains. In November, Babe's doctor sent him to the hospital where, following surgery, his illness was diagnosed as cancer. The Babe was never told but he probably knew, as did many of his fans, that he was in the ninth inning of his life.

During his convalescence more than 30,000 letters poured in wishing him well and telling him of countless prayers being said for his recovery. Millions of people around the country were deeply concerned for a ballplayer who hadn't been in a ball game for a dozen years. The Babe responded with the same old fire of competitive spirit that marked his playing days. On February 15, he was released from the hospital. The crowds that waited outside the hospital for a glimpse of the one and only Babe were shocked at his appearance. Gaunt and weak, but with unflagging spirit, the Babe waved to the crowd and went home with Claire.

Almost miraculously he began to put on weight and gain strength, and by April he was able to accept an offer of a job from the Ford Motor Company. The job called for Babe to travel around the American Legion Junior Baseball League and "appear before the boys, offer them what advice I had to give on baseball and sportsmanship and life in general, and help with league matters." "It was, and remains," he said, "the kind of job I'd always hoped I'd have, though I wish I had the strength, and authority, to expand it

to adult fans. Still, the Ford Company's act is to my mind the finest kind of public service and I'm proud to be a part of it."

Commissioner Chandler designated Sunday, April 27, 1947, "Babe Ruth Day" in every ball park in organized baseball. It was not meant as a fundraising scheme. It was to be, as Chandler said, "an expression of affection to one who has contributed so much to our national sport—baseball."

For Babe, it was one of his most thrilling experiences.

"There were nearly 60,000 in the Yankee Stadium when I walked out to home plate," he said, "and my thoughts reeled back to the day when poor old Lou Gehrig made the same hard trip from the dugout." The Babe's step was uncertain as he took his place at home plate. His voice was weak and hoarse and the once-black hair was virtually snow-white—a result of X-ray treatments.

He spoke a few words, without a script and straight from the heart. "The only real game, I think, in the world is baseball." Most of his words were directed to the "kids" of the nation. "If you try hard enough you're bound to come out on top. . . ." He finished with, "There have been so many lovely things said about me today that I'm glad to have had the opportunity to thank everybody. Thank you."

Then he walked slowly back to the dugout, followed by a thunderous ovation that crashed down on him from every corner of the mighty stadium that his homers had helped to build.

In 1948 Hollywood decided to make a movie of his life called *The Babe Ruth Story* and the Babe went out to the West Coast to serve as a technical adviser. He had made two full-length movies back in the twenties—both of which he wanted to forget—and he had had a bit part in *The Pride of the*

84

In 1948, Hollywood made a movie of Babe's life called The Babe Ruth Story. William Bendix played the part of Ruth. Above, Babe autographs baseballs for Claire Trevor, who played the part of Ruth's wife, Claire, in the movie.

Yankees, the story of Lou Gehrig, which starred Gary Cooper. In that movie he played himself.

The part of Babe Ruth in the 1948 movie was played by William Bendix, who is best remembered today for his comic television series *The Life of Riley*. The movie was not of Academy Award caliber and Babe left the New York premiere halfway through the showing.

June 13, 1948, was designated as the twenty-fifth anniversary of Yankee Stadium—The House That Ruth Built. The highlight of the ceremony was to be the permanent retirement of Babe's No. 3 uniform. No other Yankee would ever wear No. 3. It would also be the last time that Babe Ruth ever appeared in a uniform or at a ball park.

As Babe moved slowly out to home plate—the same plate where for so many years he had belted home runs—the capacity crowd stood as one to acclaim him. He had a bat in his hand but he was no longer the same power-house who had changed the concept of baseball. The once-mightiest hitter of them all was now thin and stooped—his bat almost a crutch to support his pain-wracked frame.

Ruth looked up at a sea of faces shouting out their love and affection for their one and only Babe. He took off his hat and as the thunderous applause continued unabated he bowed his head and listened to the cheers he must have known he was hearing for the last time. And then, as grown men blinked back unabashed tears, Babe Ruth turned and walked slowly to the Yankee dugout. The applause reverberated across the Harlem River to the Polo Grounds, and down to Battery Park at the tip of Manhattan. And it continued long after No. 3 was gone from the field, never to return.

Thirteen days later, Babe entered Memorial Hospital and on the night of August 16, he told Claire, "Don't come back tomorrow. I won't be here." She did come back, of course, but at 8:01 on the morning of August 17, Babe Ruth died. The man was gone, but the legend will live as long as men and boys play baseball.

The Babe lay in state in the lobby of Yankee Stadium as 100,000 fans passed by his coffin to bid farewell to the greatest sports figure of all time. The funeral services were held at St. Patrick's Cathedral and police had to turn back an overflow crowd of bereaved fans. And, as Arthur Daley reported, "It rained that day. Even the heavens wept at the passing of Babe Ruth."

The American public took Babe Ruth into their hearts as they have no other sports figure before or since. Perhaps

---

June 13, 1948, was designated as the twenty-fifth anniversary of Yankee Stadium—The House That Ruth Built. The highlight of the ceremony was the permanent retirement of Babe's No. 3 uniform. No other Yankee would ever wear No. 3. Opposite, Babe leans on a bat at home plate during the ceremony.

the secret lies in that Babe never tried to deceive his fans. His life and ways were an open book and he never learned the social grace of keeping his thoughts to himself. When he flopped on the playing field he never had an alibi; when he got in trouble off the field he never whispered. His greatness and his frailties were there for all to see.

Perhaps the secret lies in his enviable lust for life and the gusto with which he lived it to the hilt. His escapades were a constant source of news copy; rarely has the public been so well informed about the capers of a sports hero. And no matter how zealously he lived the gay life, the fans always got every nickel of their money's worth from the Babe.

Perhaps it was his rags-to-riches career that captured the fancy of the fans. His climb from a charity home to the highest salary in sports fitted well with the American dream. The public loved the big fellow, too, because he mirrored their own shortcomings, and at the same time personified the greatness most men can only dream of.

In short, Babe Ruth had the one great requisite of an American folk hero —an identity with the common man. The fans could share his triumphs and groan with him in the agonies of his occasional slumps. He won his honors as they themselves would have liked to win them and he lived his life as they would have liked to live.

And in the process, Babe Ruth made baseball history.

Two months after the anniversary of Yankee Stadium, Babe Ruth died. The funeral services were held at St. Patrick's Cathedral on August 19, 1948. Opposite, crowds line the streets to watch the casket containing Babe's body as it is taken from the hearse to be carried into the cathedral.

GEORGE HERMAN (BABE) RUTH
BOSTON–NEW YORK, A.L.; BOSTON, N.L.
1915–1935
GREATEST DRAWING CARD IN HISTORY OF
BASEBALL. HOLDER OF MANY HOME RUN
AND OTHER BATTING RECORDS. GATHERED
714 HOME RUNS IN ADDITION TO FIFTEEN
IN WORLD SERIES.

Above, the plaque honoring Babe Ruth that appears in the Baseball Hall of Fame at Cooperstown, New York. Babe was elected to the Hall of Fame in 1936.

Between Babe Ruth's first home run in 1915 and the one that cleared the grandstand roof of Forbes Field in 1935, there were 712 other home runs—a grand total of 714 such clouts. No other player has ever approached that total, and the chances are no one ever will. To accomplish such a feat a player would have to average thirty-five or more homers for twenty seasons. Some have kept up the pace for a decade, only to falter in later years. And as their quest falls short of the record established by Ruth, the world pauses to reflect once again on the greatness of the Babe.

Babe Ruth was the most colorful and exciting sports figure of his time—perhaps of all time. For twenty-two years he rode his meteoric career on a spectacular roller-coaster ride across the baseball parks of America and into the hearts of millions of fans. As long as baseball is played on city streets, in sandlots, or in big league parks, the accomplishments of Babe Ruth will serve as an inspiration to every generation of American youngsters.

He added a richness to the game of baseball such as no man has before or since. In baseball's darkest hour, following the disclosure of the infamous Black Sox Scandal in 1920, it was Babe Ruth who saved the sport from oblivion. With his mighty bat he helped erase the ugly stain of deceit and fraud from the game, for there was nothing so undeniably truthful as a "Ruthian" home run. And in the process he changed the game as drastically as the aerial pass changed the game of football. When it became evident that the fans were flocking to the parks in record numbers to see Ruth hit home runs, other players began swinging for the fences too. Thus, a new explosive spark was added to the national pastime.

At the close of his baseball career, Babe Ruth held or shared some sixty-one baseball records—many of which still stand. The thrills he provided throughout his career have rarely been equaled and can never be excelled. As one old-time ballplayer once put it, "He was just about the greatest thing that ever came to baseball. I guess you'd say that Babe Ruth is baseball."

But if Babe Ruth gave so very much to the sport, he always felt he received much more in return. From unloved street urchin and reform-school inmate he rose to become the highest-paid player of his day. "Baseball," he was to say not long before he died, "is the greatest game God ever saw fit to let man invent."

With a big fifty-two-ounce bat, an awesome natural ability and an unbridled zest for playing baseball, Babe Ruth met his destiny. More than any other single individual, the sport of baseball owes its honored place on the American scene to Babe Ruth—the "Sultan of Swat."

Bibliography

ALLEN, LEE. *100 Years of Baseball.* New York: Bartholomew House, 1950.

ALLEN, LEE and TOM MEANY. *Kings of the Diamond.* New York: G. P. Putnam's, 1965.

"Babe Ruth" *New York Times Magazine,* September 2, 1951.

————. *Saturday Review,* October 8, 1955.

————. *Newsweek,* July 14, 1934.

————. *New Yorker,* July 31, 1926.

————. *Current Biography Annual,* 1944.

————. *Literary Digest,* July 31, 1926.

BARROW, EDWARD. *My Fifty Years in Baseball.* New York: Coward McCann, 1951.

CLEVELAND, C. B. *Great Baseball Managers.* New York: Crowell, 1950.

COOK, T. R. *Essays in Modern Thought.* 1935.

CUMMINGS, PARKE, ed. *Baseball Stories.* New York: Hill and Wang, 1959.

DALEY, ARTHUR. *Kings of the Home Run.* New York: G. P. Putnam's, 1962.

FEIN, I. A. "Babe's Last Moment of Glory." *Sports Illustrated,* August 14, 1961.

FISHWICK, MARSHALL. *American Heroes: Myth and Reality.* Washington: Public Affairs Press, 1954.

FURLONG, W. B. "That Sixtieth Home Run." *New York Times Magazine,* August 20, 1961.

GALLICO, PAUL. *Farewell to Sport.* 1941.

————. "Word of Babe Ruth." (story) *Saturday Evening Post,* February 13, 1954.

GRAHAM, FRANK. *Lou Gehrig, A Quiet Hero.* New York: G. P. Putnam's, 1942.

————. *The New York Yankees.* New York: G. P. Putnam's, 1958.

HEUMAN, WILLIAMS. *Famous American Athletes.* New York: Dodd, Mead & Co., 1963.

HOYT, WAITE C. *Babe Ruth As I Knew Him.* New York: Dell Publishing Co., 1948.

JOHNSON, C. H. L. *Famous American Athletes of Today,* 1938.

KAHN, J. M. "Babe Pitching, The Babe Hitting." *Colliers,* April 22, 1950.

KETCHUM, R. M. "Faces From The Past" *American Heritage,* August, 1965. "King's Last." *Rotarian,* October, 1958.

KRUGER, JOSEPH. *Baseball's Greatest Drama.* Milwaukee, 1948.

LIEB, FRED. *Story of the World Series.* New York: G. P. Putnam's, 1949.

McGOVERN, J. T. *Diogenes Discovers Us.* 1933.

MEANY, THOMAS. *Babe Ruth; The Big Moments of the Big Fellow.* New York: Grosset, 1951.

————. *The Yankee Story.* New York: E. P. Dutton, 1960.

MORRIS, R. B. "Babe Ruth, pitcher." *New York Times Magazine,* August 10, 1958.

ORR, J. "The Girl Who Struck Out Babe Ruth." *Coronet,* June, 1959.

PIPP, W. "Bad Day for Babe Ruth," July 30, 1962.

RHODES, A. D. "Uncle Abner and the Babe." *Sports Illustrated,* May 28, 1962.

RICE, GRANTLAND. "Babe Ruth." *Coronet,* April, 1955.

————. *Tumult and the Shouting.* New York: A. S. Barnes, 1954.

RUTH, CLAIRE (MERRITT) with BILL SLOCUM. *The Babe and I.* Englewood, N. J.: Prentice-Hall, 1959.

RUTH, GEORGE HERMAN. *Babe Ruth's Own Book of Baseball.* 1928.

————. *How To Play Baseball.* 1931.

————. as told to Bob Considine. *The Babe Ruth Story.* New York: Dutton, 1948.

SCHUESSLER, R. "Home Runs: fact & fancy." *American Mercury,* July, 1956. "Speaking of pictures; old film with Babe Ruth as homer-hitting iceman." *Life,* August 28, 1950.

SMITH, IRA L. *Baseball's Famous Outfielders.* New York: A. S. Barnes, 1954.

SMITH, KEN. *Baseball's Hall of Fame.* New York: A. S. Barnes, 1947.

WELDON, MARTIN. *Babe Ruth.* New York: Crowell, 1948.

————. "The Other Side of Babe Ruth." *Coronet,* June, 1952.

Glossary

BALL—A pitched baseball that is not struck at by the batter and does not pass through the strike zone.

BASE ON BALLS—A move to first base that a batter is allowed to take when he has received four balls.

BASE PATH—The path between bases used by the runner.

BATTING AVERAGE—The percentage of times a player gets a hit. The batting average is found by dividing the number of base hits made by a player by the number of times he has been at bat. The figure is carried to three decimal places.

BULL PEN—An area at the side of the playing field where relief pitchers "warm up."

BUNT—A pitched baseball that is tapped lightly by a batter who is facing the pitcher and holding the bat in front of him.

CELLAR—Last place.

DOUBLE HEADER—Two games played one right after the other by the same teams on the same day.

DOUBLE PLAY—Two players put out during the same play.

EARNED-RUN AVERAGE—The average number of runs a pitcher allows the opposing team to score in nine innings. The earned-run average is found by dividing the number of earned runs a pitcher allows by the number of innings pitched and multiplying by nine.

ERROR—A mistake made by the defending team (the team not at bat) that allows the opponents to reach a base safely.

FLY—A baseball that is hit very high into the air; it is usually easy for a fielder to catch a fly ball, for he has time to move to where the ball will come down.

FOUL BALL—A hit ball that goes outside the area designated as fair-ball territory.

GRAND SLAM—A home run that is hit when the bases are loaded. A total of four runs score on a grand-slam homer.

GROUNDER—A baseball that touches the ground almost as soon as it has been hit by a batter.

HIT—Any ball hit by a batter that lands in fair territory and cannot be caught and thrown to first base before the batter gets there.

HOME RUN—Any hit that gives the batter time to circle the bases and return safely to home plate to score a run.

INNING—The division of baseball games in which each team has a turn at bat. A team's turn at bat ends when three men are put out. There are nine innings in a baseball game, unless the score is tied at the end of the first nine innings. In the case of a tie score, the game continues until the first inning in which one team scores more runs than the other.

LINE DRIVE—A ball that is hit straight and close to the ground.

LINEUP—The batting order of the players and the positions they will play.

MANAGER—The director of the team; he directs the play, selects the pitchers, decides the batting order, chooses the signals, etc.

OUT—The retiring of a player during his team's turn at bat. A man may be put out for any of several reasons, including the following: If he strikes out, if a ball he hits is caught after it touches the ground but is thrown to first base and caught before he gets there, or if he is tagged by a fielder with the ball when he is not touching base.

PINCH HITTER—A batter used in place of the batter next in the lineup—usually used when it is especially important for the team to get a hit.

POP FLY—A hit ball that usually goes only a short distance and flies high up into the air.

ROOKIE—A new player in baseball.

RUN—A run is scored when a player touches each base and reaches home plate without being put out by the opponents.

RUNS BATTED IN—Runs a batter scores after getting a hit, after taking a base on balls, or after being hit by a pitched ball.

SHUTOUT—A game in which one team is prevented from scoring any runs.

SOUTHPAW—A pitcher who is left-handed.

STEAL—To run safely from one base to the next without there having been a hit or an error.

STRIKE—A pitched ball that passes through the strike zone—over home plate, between the batter's shoulders and his knees—and is not struck at; any pitched ball that is struck at and missed; the first and second foul ball hit by a batter (a third foul ball hit by a batter does not count as a strike or an out unless it is bunted and caught or caught in the air).

STRIKEOUT—Three strikes called on a batter to put him out.

SWITCH-HITTER—A player who is able to hit either right-handed or left-handed.

TRIPLE PLAY—Three players put out during the same play.

UMPIRE—The official in baseball whose job it is to rule on all plays of a baseball game.

WARM UP—To practice before or during a game.

WORLD SERIES—A series of seven games played at the end of the baseball season between the major-league pennant winners to decide what team will be the professional champion.

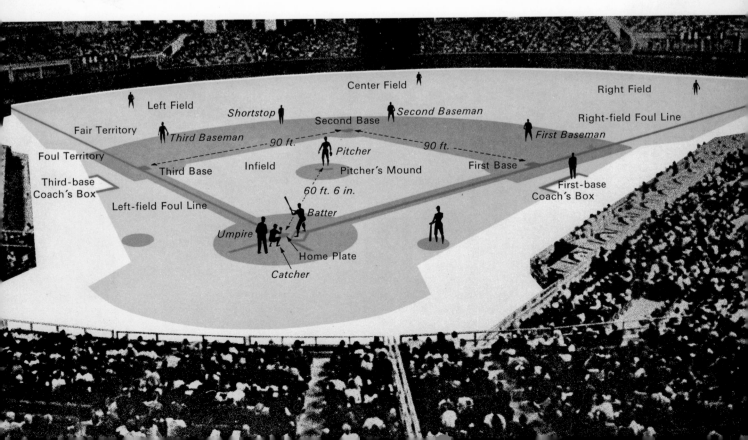

Index